A YORKSHIRE COOKBOOK

A YORKSHIRE COOKBOOK

Mary Hanson Moore

DAVID & CHARLES
Newton Abbot   London   North Pomfret (Vt)

British Library Cataloguing in Publication Data

Moore, Mary Hanson
   A Yorkshire cookbook.
   1. Cookery, English
   I. Title
   641.5'9428'1   TX717

   ISBN 0-7153-7892-9

Library of Congress Catalog Card Number: 79-56056

Typeset by ABM Typographics Limited, Hull
and printed in Great Britain
by Biddles Limited, Guildford, Surrey
for David & Charles (Publishers) Limited
Brunel House   Newton Abbot   Devon

Published in the United States of America
by David & Charles Inc
North Pomfret   Vermont 05053   USA

CONTENTS

For Fergie
eater of Fat Rascals
with love

1 When Daisy Brought The Milk

Thursdays were very special days when I was small. I lived in the West Riding of Yorkshire, in the heavy woollen district, renowned for its thick, fleecy blankets, its good cloth, and what was known as 'shoddy', for which my own town was the world's centre. Shoddy was one of the early forms of recycling, a new cloth formed from the rags of old ones. There was indeed richness in rags, and the town prospered well on its product. There was soot and dirt of course, because in those days no one cared too much about the environment; life was hard work and equally hard play, and if the work produced black grime, no one had the time to worry about that.

The work also produced good appetites, helped along by the hard climate of Yorkshire where a good 'rib-sticking' meal might ward off some of the biting east winds that whistled along the narrow valleys. And these appetites were well and truly assuaged by the cooking of the women of Yorkshire—proud, traditional cooks who learned from childhood how to make meals that would help the work go down—and always traditional meals and methods were followed. One of these traditions in my town was the Thursday Baking Day.

I can still remember the warm, spicy smells that greeted me upon my return from school, as I opened the door of the house and went inside our tiny living-room. Our back-to-back, terraced house was in a long row facing an identical row across about twenty feet of old 'setts', those square cobblestones of the North. The living-room was also the kitchen, with a small, shallow stone sink in one corner, and the 'range' in the middle of one wall.

This cast-iron range was both the pride and sorrow of my mother. It had to be blackleaded each week in order to satisfy both tradition and her own Yorkshire pride. To own such a range and not keep it gleaming was a sign of Southern decadence; everyone knew that Southerners had no pride in either themselves or their homes. I always wondered how we all knew that, since no one in my street, at any rate, had ever travelled out of Yorkshire!

On this range, my mother did all her cooking, using heavy, black, iron pans on top of the coal fire, and the oven at the side for baking. This was where the sorrow part came in, for in order to get up a good baking temperature, the fire had to be stoked at the crack of dawn and kept roaring hot, even in summer, lest the oven 'fall'. And, since the living-room opened straight out on to the street, the door hadn't to be opened widely, or closed with a bang, in case the same thing happened. The result was, each Thursday, half an hour of creeping about when I came home from school for dinner, and on my return at four o'clock, a white scrubbed wooden table laden with delicious goodies, and a mother with a headache. In those days, I didn't realise what a heavy strain those wonderful baking days put on my mother and indeed on all the housewives in the area.

Her baking tins were smooth and dulled, and she never seemed to wash them, since they had a slightly greased surface on which no cake would ever dare to stick. Most of them had belonged to her mother, and I wonder now how many new tins were ever sold in my part of the world? There were loaf tins, in two sizes, round cake tins, scores of bun tins, and of course the scrubbed, worn-down old wooden rolling pin. She had no immaculate Formica surface or marble board on which to roll out her pastry, only the wooden-topped kitchen table, uneven and ridged; her flour stayed in the paper bag in which she had bought it; and her pastry was superb.

Each Thursday, on the big table, would be spread large,

8

golden, crisp-topped loaves of bread, enough for a week's eating, for no Yorkshire housewife then would dream of buying her bread, unless in a dire emergency. There would be one large fruit-cake, redolent of cinnamon and mixed spice; trays of small buns, spotted with currants (there for my brother and his rugby-playing friends); shortcrust almond tarts, crisp and golden, with a delicious splodge of jam hidden beneath the almond mixture; saucer-sized Yorkshire curd tarts, spicy and faintly cheesy; and the large square slab of parkin, brown and sticky on top, adding its ginger scent to the rest. All this— except the parkin which was put away for a week to improve— was to be eaten the week following baking day, and sure enough, by the time it came round again, the cake tins would be empty.

There were other things too, baked for special occasions, perhaps, or for a change, or simply to use up left-over bits and pieces. 'Fat rascals' were among the latter—scraps of shortcrust pastry rolled out, sugared and sprinkled with a few currants, then rolled again into thick, flat cakes before baking. Spread with butter when hot from the oven, they were delicious. There were Yorkshire teacakes, flat thick cakes of bread enriched with currants, marvellous for toast and jam; custard pies, or egg pies as they were sometimes known, small, deep tartlets filled with a nutmeg-flavoured set custard and eaten cold; there were gingerbreads, totally different from the parkin, and with many variations; and Christmas time added to the long list, with its cakes and pies, trifles and syllabubs.

My mother believed in good food, and however short of money we might be—and we often were, especially when my father was made redundant shortly before the start of World War II— she would never save on food. Not for her the margarine, that hard yellow brick of imitation butter, and not even for cakes did she relax this rule. The first time I ever bought margarine was after war had begun, and I went to collect our week's rations. I shall never forget the look on her face as she prodded this 'excuse for butter' as she called it! Once father was out of work, she took in lodgers because, as she said, we could all eat well if she had a lot to cook for, and we did.

Each Friday, on leaving school, I had to make a detour to

call at a smallholding just out of the town. Here I waited until the owner killed two chickens. It should have put me off chicken for life, watching the poor things running about one moment, headless the next, but at that age I was more interested in the way their legs went on kicking long after their heads had gone.

On Saturday, I would be sent into the town to shop, usually for bacon, because there was more choice than in our small local corner shop. I soon learned how to tell if a bacon joint would be too salty or not. After that I would go into the big market to buy a rabbit. 'And make him turn it over so that you can see there's no shot in its back!' my mother would warn me; I would gravely ask the stallholder to do just that, before parting with my nine pennies.

My mother was a countrywoman, not born to town ways, and after marrying her soldier husband, she must have found it hard to live in the dirt and gloom of our town, but she always retained her country ways of cooking. And if sometimes, when we had been into our nearest bit of countryside for a picnic, she 'happened' to find a turnip lying loose in the field, it was only her country instinct that made her hate waste.

In the late summer evenings, when the first new potatoes reached the shops, she would sit on the doorstep, patiently scraping the little 'chats', and then boil them quickly in hot salted water. Topped with a good knob of butter, these made a wonderful supper for my brother and me after our games of 'touch and pass' or street cricket. As a rare treat, we were sometimes allowed to go to the little local pie shop for another famous West Riding dish—a 'swimmer'. This was a small meat pie, usually pork, set in a plate of thickly gooey, mushy peas. It was a winter treat, sparingly allowed because of the cost, and in the summer our treat would be a packet of small ginger snaps, with milk.

Milk was something else that my mother, as a countrywoman, believed in, and although we drank tea with our meals, there was always milk for supper. It was delivered by a burly man called Leonard, driving a two-wheeled milk float, and one of my childhood delights was to ride in this float from one end of our street to the other. Leonard would be at people's doors, pouring milk from the big churn by means of a narrow measure, but I was quite safe in the float, as his patient horse Daisy knew exactly which house he would call at, and stopped each time. I loved to watch the stream of thick white milk pour from the narrow can into a jug; the can would then be hung on the side of the churn by its curved handle. For me, then, the novelty was the small bottle of milk we had to drink each day at school, punching a hole for the straw through the cardboard top, and I used to think that only school milk came in bottles.

School dinners cost 5d a day, which was rather too much for my mother, so we would walk home at 12.30 to eat our dinner. This was always the main meal, as my father also came home from his timekeeping job at one of the mills, and we would all sit down to such things as meat and potato pie, hotpot, rabbit done in a sage sauce, ham and pea broth—so thick with bits of ham and mushy peas that the spoon would easily stand upright unaided—haslet, hash, and beef and cow-heel pie.

On Mondays, we very often had something my mother called 'collops'. These were simply big slices of raw potato, about a quarter of an inch thick, fried in dripping until deliciously golden brown, then eaten with lots of bread and butter. I imagine that the name came from the old, traditional 'Collop Monday' before Lent, when thin slices of pork or bacon were eaten to 'use up the pig'. It was a simple, quick, and extremely filling meal for mother to prepare on what was always, by tradition, washing day, when the small room would be filled with steam, from the 'copper' boiling on the fire—a big zinc bucket in which all the white clothes had to be boiled in order to reach the required standard of West Riding whiteness. There were no amazing packets of biological this-and-that in those days.

Sometimes though, the dinner would be Monday Hash instead—a mixture of potatoes, onions and corned beef slices. My father always left his bits of corned beef, because he used to say that he had eaten so much of it during the Great War that he never wanted to see it again.

* * *

The rest of the week, after the washing was done, saw a gradual improvement in the dinners. There might be Ham Pestil on Tuesdays if mother had managed to scrounge a ham bone from our little corner shop. Fry was another great favourite, a mix of pig's fry cooked slowly in the side oven, or Yorkshire Beef Collops which were quite different from the washing-day ones. Meat and Tatie Pie was a sturdy West Riding favourite; for this, topped with mother's fine pastry, it was well worth running the two miles home from school.

MONDAY HASH

Slice peeled potatoes and onions thinly, layer in a large frying pan, season and add a little water. Cover, and cook slowly until almost soft, then place slices of corned beef on top and finish cooking.

FRY

1½lb fry (mixture of pig's heart,   *1 level teaspoon each sage,*
   liver, kidney, sweetbread and   *thyme, marjoram*
   stewing meat) thinly sliced   *salt and pepper*
1lb onions, chopped   *1 pint water*

Cook all together, very slowly, in a covered casserole until the meat is tender.

Two more recipes using pig's fry, are also simple.

FRY PUDDING

Cut a pig's fry into thin slices, season well and layer in a basin with slices of onion. Add a little water and cover with a good suet crust. Steam for 2 hours.

FRY

2lb fry   *2oz dripping*
2oz seasoned flour   *water*

Cut the fry into small pieces, roll in the flour. Place in a greased tin, with sufficient water to come halfway up the meat pieces. Dot with dripping and bake at 350° (Mark 4). Thicken the pan juices, if liked, with cornflour.

HASLET

This is another recipe calling for a pig's fry, or Pluck, as it is sometimes called. Haslet is sold all over the North in pork butchers' shops, but it is also a very easily made delicacy.

1lb cleaned fry
1lb minced pork, a mixture of
   fat and lean
1½lb onions, finely chopped
½ teaspoon sage

salt and pepper
1 pig's caul
2oz lard

Chop or mince the fry, mix with pork, onions, sage and seasoning. Wrap in the caul, put in a greased roasting dish and dot with lard. Bake in a hot oven until well browned.

This is a very old recipe and pigs' cauls are not easily come by now, unless you are a farmer, so the mixture can be put straight into a suitably sized tin, to form a flat cake. This is how it is now sold in the shops.

YORKSHIRE BEEF COLLOPS

2lb minced beef
½lb onions, finely chopped
2oz dripping
salt and pepper
pinch of ground nutmeg

¾ pint stock
1 bundle herbs
2 tablespoons brown sauce
12oz pearl barley, softened
   overnight in water

Fry the onion and mince in the dripping. Season, add the nutmeg, stock and herbs. Simmer for 40 minutes, add the sauce and barley. Mix well and cook for 10 minutes. Serve on a dish with a border of mashed potatoes.

* * *

Another way of using offal is a very old one that Grandma passed on to me. This combined meat and fruit as an Indian curry does, and was always a mystery to me!

SWEET POTS

2 cups coarse oatmeal
2 cups cooked liver, lights and
  heart, chopped
1 handful currants and sultanas,
  mixed

salt and pepper
pinch of ground nutmeg

Scald the oatmeal with boiling water, leave to swell. Mix with the meat, fruits, nutmeg and seasoning, put into a greased basin and steam for 45 minutes. Serve with mashed potatoes and turnips.

*   *   *

A turnip, by the way, in the West Riding of Yorkshire as in Scotland, is the round orange vegetable known as a swede by Southern people. And a good way with turnip is one using a sausage stuffing.

STUFFED TURNIPS

Wash and peel 3 turnips (or swedes!). Scoop out the middles. Season with salt and pepper, and fill with sausage meat. Put into a steamer and cover with greased greaseproof paper. Steam for 1½ hours, until tender. Serve with a plain white sauce.

*   *   *

Still on the offal trail, another great Yorkshire favourite is Yorkshire Goose.

YORKSHIRE GOOSE

1½lb ox liver
1oz seasoned flour
1lb onions, sliced
melted butter

salt and pepper
sage to season
¾ pint stock or water
1lb potatoes, sliced

Clean the liver and wipe dry. Cut into thin slices and coat with flour. Lightly fry the onions in melted butter, then put into a dish with the liver, sprinkling each layer with salt, pepper and sage. Pour on the stock or water and cover with the sliced potatoes. Cover and bake for 1 hour in a moderate oven. Take off the lid for the last 20 minutes to brown the potatoes.

* * *

One of the great traditional dishes of Yorkshire and of Lancashire too, is the Black Pudding. Made from the pig's blood, mixed with delicious morsels of pork fat, and skilfully seasoned, it is comparable with any sausage made on the Continent—if you are a true-blooded Yorkshireman!

The blood must be freshly drawn as soon as the pig is killed, and stirred to prevent clotting, though in some recipes it is left to stand overnight and the thin part drawn off the next day.

BLACK PUDDING (also known as HOG'S PUDDING)

1 pint fresh pig's blood	*¼ level teaspoon pepper*
4oz pearl barley	*8oz pork fat, diced*
4oz fine oatmeal	*2oz onion, finely chopped*
1oz salt	*clean intestine skins*

Cook the barley in 4 times its own volume of water until just soft. Mix the oatmeal with the salt and pepper and make a paste with a little strained blood. Add the barley, pork fat, onion and the rest of the strained blood. Either put into skins through a funnel, stirring all the time, or into a greased baking tin. If in skins, tie loosely and drop the puddings into hot water. Boil for 20 minutes. The puddings are ready if no blood comes out when they are gently pricked. If in a tin, bake the pudding for 45 minutes.

They can be eaten cold, or warmed through and served with mashed potatoes, or grilled or fried for breakfast. Delicious! The older recipes sometimes add shredded green of leek, and eggs. They are extremely nutritious, and the perfect answer after those great fell walks.

For the days when money was not too short, a treat of kidneys was offered, eked out in mother's economical way by a delicious coating of pastry.

SAVOURY PATTIES

Slice lamb's kidneys thinly, season with mace, salt and pepper, and enclose in puff pastry. Bake in a hot oven until the pastry is golden brown.

* * *

And still with the offal, is the recipe for Yorkshire Ducks.

YORKSHIRE DUCKS

1lb pig's fry, including the caul	*3oz breadcrumbs*
½ teaspoon salt	*½ teaspoonsage*
3 medium onions	*½ teaspoon dried mixed herbs*

Soak the caul in salted water. Wash the fry, peel the onions and put both into a saucepan with just enough salted water to cover. Simmer for 45 minutes. Remove from the heat, drain off the liquid, pouring a little on to the breadcrumbs, and saving the rest for gravy. Mince the fry and chop the onions, add seasonings and moistened breadcrumbs. Beat all together, adding a little more liquid if too dry. Cut the caul into 4in squares, and put 2 tablespoons of the mixture on to each square. Make into balls. Put these on to a greased baking tin with the joined edges underneath to stop the mixture coming out. Cook quickly in a hot oven for 20 minutes. Make a good thick gravy with the remaining liquid.

* * *

On Saturday afternoons, my mother would take me to the local cinema matinee. My brother came too, until he grew too big to be seen out with the females! For 9d I would sit in the warm darkness, feeling the strangely prickly red plush seats, eyes glued to the screen as my heroes and heroines acted out their stories. I sat through all the 'oldies', and even the epics, such as

Frankenstein and Dracula, and after my mother had told me that 'it was all just a story', I never seemed to suffer from nightmares or bad dreams. (But I hated having to go down into the big cellars to fetch coal, and would run like mad back up into the daylight!)

After the show had ended, we would wander about the busy Saturday market, where the wind made the canvas stall-covers flap loudly, and in winter, the spluttering gas lights threw pools of yellow welcome amongst the jostling crowds. We would stand and listen to the patter, the man selling crockery, skilfully piling it up along one arm, throwing plates about with never a smash; and the medicine man, offering his great cure-all, to the amusement of the large crowd listening. But as soon as he started talking about the price of his medicine, the crowd would melt away as if by magic and he would begin his tale again.

There would be cheap cuts of meat on offer, for refrigeration was scarce in those days and the stallholders were anxious to get rid of their goods before the market closed. Vegetables too would be almost given away, and sometimes my mother would take advantage of this, but she always tried to hurry such transactions because she liked to think that we were not quite as poor as that!

And before we turned for home, there would be the tripe shop to visit, to buy something for father's tea. He loved tripe, and we always had it for Saturday tea. Thick yellow seam tripe, the white flopping honeycomb, and elder, also yellow and cut like a cake in big slices, there was the brown sausage-shaped tripe too, intestines of course, but I never knew the name—they were all delicious, seasoned with salt and pepper, and sprinkled with malt vinegar.

FRICASSEE OF TRIPE

Cut white seam tripe into long pieces and put into a pan with some good gravy, a few breadcrumbs, a lump of butter, vinegar to taste, and a little mustard. Add a little chopped parsley and simmer slowly until tender.

* * *

Sometimes, as a special treat, mother would buy cow heels, and I would enjoy chewing at the big bones. There was another way of eating them, instead of just plain boiled. This was to cut the boiled heels into pieces, dip them into beaten egg then flour, then fry them until golden brown. With fried onions they were wonderful!

2 Tatie Pie On Thursdays

Perhaps it is just the natural, inborn economy of the Yorkshire housewife, or it may be that for the whole length of our native Pennine hills sheep graze in their thousands, but the fact is there: in Yorkshire, the sheep—be it called mutton or lamb— figures large in the eating. And hardly any of it is thrown away. The same is true in Lancashire, particularly those parts of the county that encroach upon the Pennines, and this, along with the same tradition that wives went out to work, has meant the long survival of that most delicious food—hotpot.

Historically, it belongs to Lancashire, where the mill lasses would put a combination of mutton, potatoes and onions into the oven at the crack of dawn, go and work all day in the clattering cotton mills, and come home to a rich meal in the evening. But in Yorkshire, too, women ran the big woollen looms, and many of them were wives with families to feed; similarly, the long slow oven cooking is necessary.

YORKSHIRE HOTPOT

2lb best end neck of mutton
2lb potatoes, sliced
2lb onions, sliced

stock or water
1oz butter
salt and pepper

Layer the meat with the potatoes and onions in a tall cook pot.
Add about 1 pint stock or water and put the butter on top.
Season. Cover tightly and cook in a slow oven for 3 to 4 hours.
Remove the lid for the last 30 minutes to let the potatoes brown.

LITTLE MUTTON PIES

1lb lean mutton or lamb
3 medium onions
salt and pepper
½ pint water

1oz plain flour
1 tablespoon chopped parsley
12oz shortcrust pastry
1 egg, beaten

Dice the meat. Peel and chop the onions. Put into a pan with
seasoning and water. Bring to the boil, simmer until tender.
Blend the flour with 4 tablespoons cold water, add to pan and
reboil. Remove from heat, cool and mix in the parsley. Line 12
patty tins with pastry, reserving some for the lids. Put filling
into each, press on the lids. Make a hole in the centre of each lid
and brush with beaten egg. Bake for 20 minutes in a hot oven.

A strange-sounding dish, Fackle, probably derives from the Norwegian one called *Faa r-i-kaal*, and shows how the Scandinavian invasion of Yorkshire has left its mark. It has had a strong influence upon the Yorkshire dialect, for instance, a beck, a small mountain stream is also called that in Norway. Names and endings to names have come down straight through the centuries. This dish is good for keeping out the cold.

FACKLE

2lb scrag end of mutton	*salt and pepper to taste*
4lb firm white cabbage	*12 peppercorns*
4 tablespoons flour	*1 pint water*

Cut the meat into small pieces, leaving bones intact. Cut the cabbage into big chunks, removing the stalk. Put the meat and cabbage in layers into a big pan, sprinkling each layer with flour and seasonings. Add the water and boil for 1 hour at least, but it can be left longer. Serve with boiled potatoes.

SHEEP'S HEAD PIE

Soak a sheep's head overnight in cold salted water. Next day, clean away any blood, put into fresh cold water and bring to the boil. Leave in the water until cool enough to handle, then take out the brains. Put the head into fresh cold water, sufficient to cover, and boil for 3 hours, until the bones slip out easily. Let it cool, reserving the liquid in which it boiled. Take off the fat, cut up the meat into small pieces and lay in a pie dish with a layer of chopped parsley and seasoning. Skin the tongue and palate, cut into strips and mix with the rest of the meat. Slice 2 hard-boiled eggs and lay the slices on top of the meat. Fill up with the reserved liquid and cover with a good layer of shortcrust pastry. Bake until golden brown.

BAKED SHEEP'S HEAD 1

Boil a sheep's head in just enough water to cover. When tender, drain and bone it. Cut the meat into pieces, lay them separately on a greased baking sheet, season and sprinkle with chopped parsley and shallots, and a few drops of lemon juice. Add small pieces of dripping and a layer of browned breadcrumbs. Bake for 10 minutes in a moderate oven. Serve on mashed potatoes with gravy and tomato sauce.

BAKED SHEEP'S HEAD 2

1 sheep's head	*1 teaspoon sweet herbs*
salt	*knob of butter*
dripping	*salt and pepper*

Split the head, remove the tongue and brains. Soak the head in warm water and salt. Tie the halves together, then bake in a medium hot oven for 2 hours, basting with dripping. Potatoes can be baked with it. Boil the tongue separately until tender. Make a sauce by boiling the brains, then mashing them with herbs, butter and seasoning; stir together over a gentle heat. Place the brain sauce round the tongue, serve separately with the head.

STUFFED SHEEP'S HEAD

1 sheep's head, cooked and	*breadcrumbs*
boned as in previous recipe	*melted dripping*
savoury stuffing	

Lay half of the meat on a greased baking tin, spread with the stuffing, cover with the rest of the meat. Brush with melted dripping and sprinkle with breadcrumbs. Bake for 15 minutes. Garnish with the sliced tongue and brains, and serve with a thick gravy made from the water in which the head was cooked.

SHEEP'S TONGUES

2 sheep's tongues	*beaten egg*
salt and pepper	*breadcrumbs*
flour	

Soak the tongues in cold salted water for 3 hours. Wash in clean water then cook very slowly in enough clean water to cover.

When tender, skin and trim them, then slice lengthways into halves. Season, coat with flour, brush with beaten egg and roll in breadcrumbs. Fry in hot fat until golden brown. Serve on mashed potatoes.

MUTTON BROTH

1lb scrag mutton, cut into small
    pieces
1 quart water
good pinch of salt

1 leek, 1 carrot, 1 piece turnip,
1 stalk celery, chopped
1½ dessertspoons rice
1½ teaspoons chopped parsley

Chop the vegetables into small pieces. Put the mutton and salt into the water, bring to the boil and skim. Add the vegetables and rice, simmer for 2 hours. Skim again, remove the bones and add the parsley. Season again if necessary.

SHEEP'S HEAD BROTH

1 sheep's head, soaked overnight
    in strong salt water
1 small turnip
1lb carrots

1 stick celery
3 tablespoons barley
salt and pepper

Put the head into a large pan. Chop the vegetables into small pieces and add to the pan with the barley. Season and cover with fresh water. Bring to the boil, skim, then simmer for at least 3 hours.

STUFFED ONIONS, USING LAMB'S KIDNEYS

2 large onions
2 lamb's kidneys
1oz butter

salt and pepper
stock

Parboil the onions. Slice the kidneys and quickly brown them in the butter to seal them. Remove the centre of the onions and fill with sliced kidney. Season. Stand the onions in a dish, pour stock around them. Cover and cook in a hot oven for about 1 hour until soft.

23

SHEEP'S HEART

Wash the heart free of blood, then dry. Remove the 'deaf ears' (gristle and ends of tubes) and cut through the division in the middle. Fill the cavity with a good onion stuffing and tie grease-proof paper over to hold this in. Dust with flour, add dripping and bake for 40 minutes to 2 hours, depending on the size of the heart. Baste frequently and serve with a good thick gravy.

TROTTERS

Blanch 2 sheep's, calf's or pig's trotters, then cook in stock for 2 to 3 hours, until the bones slip out easily. Press the meat between 2 plates until cold, then dip in beaten egg and bread-crumbs and fry until golden brown. Delicious served hot with vegetables, or cold with salad.

HARICOT MUTTON

2lb best end of neck	*salt and pepper*
1oz dripping	*1 pint warm water*
1 onion, sliced	*½ tablespoon flour*
1 carrot, 1 turnip, chopped	

Cut the meat into small pieces, removing any gristle and most of the fat. Fry quickly in hot dripping, remove to another pan. Fry the onion in the fat, adding the vegetables. Allow to sweat a little, then add them to the meat. Season, add the water and simmer gently for 2 hours, skimming off the fat. Mix the flour with a little cold water, stir into the meat and vegetables, and cook for a few more minutes.

SAVOURY SHEEP'S TROTTERS

6 trotters	*salt and pepper*
½ onion, chopped	*forcemeat, about 6 tablespoons*
1 sprig parsley, chopped	*breadcrumbs*
2oz dripping	*1 teaspoon vinegar*
½ pint stock	*½oz cheese, grated*

Boil the trotters until tender. Fry the onion and parsley in the dripping, then add the stock. Season and simmer for 30 minutes. Remove bones from the trotters, place a little forcemeat in the cavities. Lay the trotters on a dish and cover with breadcrumbs. Add the vinegar to the onion gravy, pour over the trotters. Sprinkle again with breadcrumbs, and with the cheese. Brown under a grill and serve very hot.

✳   ✳   ✳

On Sundays and high days, we enjoyed better fare—a joint roasted in the oven—and although we did eat leg of mutton and pork too, the great Sunday dinner in Yorkshire was of course the roast beef of England. All along the street, as father and my brother and I returned from our Sunday morning walk, there would come wafting the delicious smells of sirloins and topsides, roasting to succulent browny-redness in the small side ovens.

We were always banished for a walk, simply to give mother more room in which to prepare the dinner; and it was more than our lives were worth to return too soon to the house; even in the cold of winter we would all tramp around, trying desperately not to look at clocks too much on the way. In summer, after spending our traditional halfpenny in the sweetshop, in which we could spend ages browsing amongst the tall glass jars full of boiled sweets and toffees, we would usually go to the allotments, where the men would be busily working on their small patches of land. Most of our small terraced houses had no gardens, and these allotments were a way of giving space and a chance to grow vegetables, to men who spent their working days in the hot mills and down the coalmines.

Although they did grow some vegetables, most of the men took great pride in growing some special flower—the lupin, or very often, the chrysanthemum. It was strange to see how gently the rough hands would hold the huge blooms for me to look at, and although the men competed with each other in trying to grow the biggest flowers, they would praise each other's blooms and help each other with the hard digging. Father had lost a leg in the Great War, and so could not garden, but he enjoyed sitting and talking to the men. During winter it

25

was a different story, and we would all wander about the town, looking in the shop windows, trying to keep warm, until it was time to go home.

There we would all sit in the hot kitchen-living-room, with mother, red-faced from her exertions, dishing up the succulent meat and its accompanying potatoes and vegetables. It was a miracle to see the golden roast potatoes and nicely cooked vegetables emerge from the old iron pans, all balanced and crowded on top of the small fire; and if mother's temper was never too good, it was not altogether surprising, considering the very difficult circumstances under which she had to cook.

One of the best parts of this Sunday dinner was of course 't' pudding'. We didn't mean the dessert, 'afters' or sweet: we meant The Pudding—the golden-brown, puffed-up, crispy-topped, soft-hearted Yorkshire Pudding. Roast beef without it would have been unthinkable. Traditionally cooked in the roasting tin that held all the meat juices and fat, this was the peak of mother's Sunday, and woe betide anyone who opened the door when it was in the oven. For any sudden draughts or jolts could cause the pudding to collapse upon itself and become a flat, sorry excuse for a 'Yorkshire'.

When it was done we made haste to the table, for a good Yorkshire must never be kept waiting. We ate it as a first course with plenty of the good beef gravy, and pepper and salt. This was of course a relic of the old hungry days when meat was expensive for large families, and so the children were first filled up with Yorkshire. Even now, I hate to be served my Yorkshire Pudding with the meat and vegetables; it is too glorious a dish, if cooked properly, to share a dinner plate. But it *must* be cooked properly, and there are many, many recipes, all slightly different, handed down within families as to the best way of doing it. Some advocate making the batter at least an hour before baking; some say use only water, others a mix of milk and water; beat it at least 15 minutes; do not overbeat; use a fork to whisk, use a whisk, use a wooden spoon—and so it goes on. But there is one sure thing; it must always be made in a large baking tin, and never in those small round bun tins that restaurants are so fond of! A piece of Yorkshire must *be* a piece, a nice large square, with at least one thick, crisp edge to soak up the gravy, and none of the fiddly little rounds so often served outside Yorkshire.

Here is my own family recipe.

YORKSHIRE PUDDING

3oz plain flour (never self-
    raising!)
½ teaspoon salt

2 eggs
½ pint milk
dripping

Put the flour and salt into a basin. Make a well in the centre and drop in the eggs. Gradually stir in the flour with a fork, mixing with the eggs and making a smooth paste. Add the milk gradually, making sure there are no lumps, then beat like a maniac until the mixture is like smooth runny cream, and the top is full of air bubbles. Heat some dripping, with some of the meat juices, until it is smoking hot, then pour in the batter. Bake in a very hot oven, about 425°F (Mark 7) until well risen and golden. (And don't open the oven door for at least 20 minutes).

* * *

Once the Sunday dinner was eaten, the remaining meat was used for several dinners during the week. Quite often, slices of the cold beef were also eaten for tea on Sundays, and a delicious home-made salad would accompany this.

A SALAD FOR COLD ROAST BEEF

Mix finely shredded lettuce with very thin onion rings, a little sugar and vinegar. Allow to stand at least 30 minutes before using.

* * *

The cold meat could also be used for another 'hash'.

HASH

1lb cold cooked beef, thinly
sliced
some beef bones
1 carrot, 1 turnip, chopped
1 pint water
pinch of dried mixed herbs

dripping
1 onion, chopped
1 level tablespoon flour
1 tablespoon Yorkshire Relish
salt and pepper

Make a stock with the bones, carrot, turnip, herbs and water, cooking for 1½ hours. Meanwhile, fry the chopped onion in dripping until brown, then stir in the flour gradually. Add the sauce and seasoning. Add the strained stock gradually, stirring well. Put in the slices of meat and heat well. (Yorkshire Relish is Yorkshire's answer to Worcester!)

* * *

Brisket was another favourite joint of meat, usually intended to be eaten cold in summer.

BRAISED BRISKET

3½lb middle cut of brisket
1 tablespoon dripping
1 small onion
8 carrots, other root vegetables
if liked

salt and pepper
good pinch of dried mixed herbs
few potatoes
½ pint water

Brown the meat in the melted dripping. Remove meat, then brown the onion and root vegetables, after chopping them into small pieces. Season, replace the meat on top of the vegetables and add the herbs. Cover with small slices of potato, add the water. Cover tightly, bring to simmering. Braise slowly for 2 to 3 hours.

This was first served warm with the vegetables, then the remaining meat was pressed between two plates until cold, for slicing.

With these joints of beef would go a fine mustard sauce, always made the day before it was to be eaten.

TRADITIONAL YORKSHIRE MUSTARD

Mix 2 parts dry English mustard and 8 parts caster sugar with enough malt vinegar to make a smooth paste.

* * *

Roast pork was a rarer treat, and usually reserved for Christmas, as a Boxing Day dinner, although sometimes we would have pork chops. Pork meat was bought from the pork butcher, a specialist shop selling every possible food made from the pigs. Haslet was obtainable there, also some strange delights known as chitterlings, which were the small intestines of the pig made into sausages filled with a mince mixture of fry. There would be scratchings, which were nothing more than crunchy pieces of fat and crackling that remain after fat has been rendered down. These were delicious, and very cheap. Pig's trotters, or pettitoes, were bought there, to be made into a lovely teatime treat (the good old Yorkshire high tea).

PETTITOES

Allow one trotter per person, split into 2 by the butcher. Wash well, put into a pan with 2 sliced onions, salt, pepper, a pinch of nutmeg and a piece of lemon peel. Add 1 pint water and boil for at least $2\frac{1}{2}$ hours. Serve with parsley sauce and bread and butter.

PORK CHAPS

These are the pig's cheeks, boiled first then brushed with breadcrumbs and roasted. They can be eaten hot or cold, and are usually already roasted when sold in Yorkshire.

* * *

In the Dales country, which I found during my teens as a keen youth hosteller, the farmer's pig was the source of much of his winter food and nearly every part of the animal could be used. Nowadays the trend is towards leaner pigs, but in older times the pig supplied good fatty bacon that helped to keep out the cold when ploughing. Hams would hang from the farmhouse rafters, and Yorkshire ham is world-famous. The original York ham was supposed to have been so named because it was believed to have been smoked in the sawdust left after building York Minster! The gammon rasher is also famous throughout Yorkshire, and a good Yorkshire high tea would start off with a thick piece of gammon fried with eggs. Nearly every farmhouse would produce a meal like this when I first started walking in the Dales, but now the cost of such a meal is too high and not many farmers' wives are able to produce it with such frequency.

At the pork butcher's shop, we would also buy pies. These were of two varieties: the cold 'Stand Pie', or the hot pie, sold with gravy. For the latter a jug was a necessary thing, as the gravy was sold hot, ready for use with the pies. The cold pie, the Stand or Pork Pie, is the backbone of a Yorkshire Christmas.

YORKSHIRE STAND PIE

2lb pork meat, minced   *1 egg, beaten*
2oz lard   *salt and pepper*
2oz butter   *½ teaspoon chopped sage*
¼ pint hot water   *pork bones*
12oz sifted flour

Melt the lard and butter in the hot water. Boil, then take from the heat. Pour the liquid into the flour, mixing quickly, adding the beaten egg. Shape up a pie crust, either by hand or round a cake tin. Reserve some pastry for a lid.

Add the seasoning and sage to the minced meat, fill the pastry case and put on the lid. Make a hole in the centre of the lid. Meanwhile, boil the bones to make a good jellying stock. When the pie is baked, about 2 hours at 350°F (Mark 4), pour warm stock into it. Leave until quite cold.

BOILED HAM

Soak the cured ham overnight. Scrape the skin clean and trim off the excess fat. Put into fresh cold water, then boil for 25 minutes to each lb, plus an extra 25 minutes (begin timing when it actually boils). Simmer gently. The addition of a pint of beer greatly improves the flavour. Before serving, remove the skin and cover the fatty surface with browned breadcrumbs.

BAKED HAM

Soak overnight. Make a crust from 2lb flour and 1 pint water. Wrap the ham in this, sealing tightly. Put in a baking tin and bake for 25 minutes to each lb, plus 25 minutes extra. When cooked, remove crust and skin, then score lines in a criss-cross fashion all over the fat. Dot with cloves, then return to the oven to brown the fat.

YORKSHIRE SAUSAGE ROLL

1lb lean pork
1lb ham
1lb fresh breadcrumbs

salt and pepper
pinch of cayenne, pinch of mace
3 eggs, lightly beaten

Mince the pork and ham finely, mix with the breadcrumbs and add the seasonings. Bind the mixture with the beaten eggs. Shape into a roll, tie into a floured cloth and boil for 3 hours. Serve cold.

HAM ROLY

8oz flour
4oz suet
½ teaspoon baking powder
pinch of salt

milk to mix
8oz ham scraps, minced
2 onions, minced
salt and pepper

Make a not too thick dough with the flour, suet, baking powder, salt and milk. Roll out into an oblong shape. Mix the ham, onions, salt and pepper, and spread on to the dough. Roll up and tie in a floured cloth. Steam for 2½ hours.

31

The bacon produced some good high teas, not just served with eggs, but made into such delectable dishes as Medley Pie.

MEDLEY PIE

6 slices of fat bacon

2 onions, sliced

1 dessertspoon dried sage

2 apples, peeled and quartered

½ cup water

shortcrust pastry

Line a pie dish with the bacon, cover with onions and add the sage, and season. Cover with apples, sweetened to taste. Add the water, cover with pastry and bake until nicely browned.

BACON CUSTARD

This is really a French quiche, but what's in a name among cooks? Line a pie dish with shortcrust pastry, put in some chopped, cooked, streaky bacon. Make a custard with 1 egg and ½ pint milk, season with salt and pepper. Pour over the bacon and bake until set.

* * *

Good pastry was something that a true Yorkshirewoman could be proud of, and its filling nature helped along the meat for big families. On Thursdays, after my trot homewards from school, I was invariably greeted by the rich smell of baking—and Meat and Tatie Pie.

MEAT AND TATIE PIE

1lb shin beef, cut into small pieces

1 large onion, cut up

2lb potatoes

shortcrust pastry

salt and pepper

Simmer the beef, onion and seasoning in water for 1½ hours until tender. Strain, reserving the stock. Boil the potatoes, cut into chunks, add to the meat. Put into a pie dish, add a little stock, then cover with fairly thick shortcrust pastry and bake in a hot oven for 40 minutes. Use the remaining meat stock to make a gravy.

Another favourite of my father's was Beefsteak and Cow Heel Pie.

BEEFSTEAK AND COW HEEL PIE

1½lb lean stewing steak, cut   *1 cow heel*
into small pieces   *stock or water*
seasoned flour   *1lb shortcrust pastry*

Dip the meat into the flour, place in a pie dish. Wash the cow heel in salted water, cut into small pieces and add to the meat. Add a little stock or water, cover with shortcrust pastry. Bake for 30 minutes in a hot oven, then cover the pastry with wet greaseproof paper, and bake on until the meat is tender (about 1½ hours).

BEEF COLLOPS

8 thin slices rump steak about   *1 teaspoon capers*
3in long   *6 or 7 shallots, shredded*
flour   *4 small gherkins*
1oz butter   *salt and pepper*
½ walnut, chopped   *some good gravy*

Beat out the slices of steak, flour them, then fry quickly for 2 minutes in the butter. Place the meat in a pan, cover with a good gravy. Add the rest of the ingredients and heat through without boiling.

YORKSHIRE OYSTERS (a very old recipe indeed)

2lb thick end leg of veal   *pinch each of ground mace and*
1lb beef suet   *nutmeg*
1 small cup breadcrumbs   *dripping*
2 eggs   *capers*
salt and pepper   *chopped mushrooms*

Skin the veal, then mince it with the suet. Add the breadcrumbs, eggs and seasonings, and mix well. Make into small flat cakes, fry in dripping. Serve with thick gravy, garnished with capers and chopped mushrooms.

And another way with veal (but not a working farmer's!) was Yorkshire Veal and Oysters.

YORKSHIRE VEAL AND OYSTERS

2lb fillet veal, cut into 8 slices,   *2oz butter*
   each about ½in thick   *beaten egg*
16 oysters   *breadcrumbs*
seasoned flour   *lemon*

Remove the oysters from their shells, save the liquid. Make a slit in each piece of veal, then stuff with 2 oysters to each piece. Dust with seasoned flour, coat with beaten egg and breadcrumbs. Fry in butter until the meat is tender, and the outside golden brown. Make a gravy with the oyster liquid and pan juices. Serve garnished with lemon.

*　*　*

In the days before freezers, whenever a beast was slaughtered, the meat had to be pickled and an old recipe for such a pickle was called, simply, Pickle.

PICKLE FOR HAMS, TONGUES AND BEEF, YORKSHIRE FASHION

1lb common salt   *8oz bay salt*
1½lb soft brown sugar   *2oz pepper*
2oz saltpetre

Rub the meat well with the common salt and leave overnight. Next day, rub in the other ingredients, then leave the meat for 3 weeks, protected from flies.

*　*　*

Rabbit was a cheap alternative for meat in our household, in the days before the dread myxomatosis disease struck our English bunnies, and after I had bought one in the market it would be served up as Savoury Rabbit.

MOTHER'S SAVOURY RABBIT

*1 young rabbit, washed and
  jointed
4 large onions, chopped
3in round from 2lb loaf of bread
  (or old crusts)*

*sage
salt and pepper
3oz bacon fat*

Leave the rabbit in salted water for 30 minutes. Cover the onions with salted water, bring to the boil. Strain off the water and reserve for gravy. Cover the bread with cold water, then squeeze out. Leave this soaked bread in rough pieces in a basin, add the cooked onions, sage to taste, salt and pepper, and bacon fat. Mix well. Put the rabbit joints into a greased baking tin and cover them with the stuffing mix. Bake in a hot oven, covering the tin for the first hour, then removing the cover for the second hour.

* * *

RABBIT PUDDING

Cut a small rabbit into small pieces. Line a basin with suet crust, and put in the rabbit pieces with small pieces of bacon or ham, seasoned to taste. Add 1 cup water. Cover with a suet crust lid, pinching well together. Boil for 2 hours.

* * *

WAKEFIELD RABBIT

*2 jointed rabbits
seasoned flour
2 eggs, beaten
1 dessertspoon dried mixed herbs*

*4oz dry breadcrumbs
dripping
cayenne pepper
salt*

Dust the joints with seasoned flour, dip into beaten egg, then coat with herbs and breadcrumbs. Melt the dripping in a baking tin, place the rabbit joints in the tin and sprinkle with cayenne and salt. Roast in a medium-hot oven for 1½ to 2 hours, basting occasionally.

Wakefield was the County town of the old West Riding of Yorkshire, a bustling town whose name means 'the field by the wayside', and can therefore be pictured as a place of rabbits scuttling about!

*　　*　　*

Of course the farmers had even more choice, but one game recipe that comes back to me from my childhood is grandma's Buttered Grouse.

Grandfather was a countryman who thought nothing of walking five miles there and back to see his grandchildren each Friday afternoon, when he would bestow a penny upon my brother and me, kiss us with his gingery-whiskered face—and I could never understand why his hair was white and his moustache ginger—and tell us to be good and go to Sunday school. We never did of course, because mother didn't believe in sending a child who had been in school all week to another form of school on Sundays. And she had a great row one day with our local Minister, who, good chapel man that he was, called her a heathen! But grandfather was chapel and no mistake, and each Sunday would see him in his pew at the little grey stone building down the road from his house. He never remembered the words of the hymns, and so would 'pom-pom' all the way through them.

He lived on the outskirts of the town, a small single street of houses clinging to the edge of the deep valley that held the town proper, and to me, that bare hillside with its small grey houses was country.

From him, I learnt two 'smells'. One, of game hanging behind the scullery door, richly wafting its strong aroma through the small house; and one of cheese—not ordinary cheese, but the powerful scent of strong Gorgonzola.

As grandfather's birthday was on Boxing Day, the whole family used to meet at his house to celebrate another year. This meant my mother and father, my brother and I, and my aunt and uncle, grandfather's son from Ilkley. And each year, as long as I remember, there would be a fat bird hanging in all its feathers behind the scullery door. (In Yorkshire, many of the houses had sculleries—they were a kind of small, extra kitchen, an annexe off the main living kitchen, where the old stone sink was put, thus making such houses a little superior.) Every time the connecting door between this small place and the main kitchen-living-room was opened, around Christmas time, the strong gamey odour would waft through. Not for years after I had grown up was I able to face cooked game dishes!

The rich Gorgonzola that he loved, made its appearance at the high tea following the Rugby match of Boxing Day afternoon, and for a long time I associated its strange smell with my brother's feet, since I knew him to suffer quite badly from smelly feet—so badly in fact that upon joining the Scots Guards later in the war, he was forcibly ejected from the sleeping-quarters by his fellow men! Only in later years, when I began to travel and to acquire more knowledge of different foods, did I realise that the strange smell at grandfather's tea table was cheese from Italy. I sent a silent, loving apology to a grave in Anzio.

BUTTERED GROUSE FROM THE MOORS

4 grouse   *salt, pepper, cayenne pepper*
blades of mace   *8oz butter*
4oz pork fat

Put a blade of mace on each bird's breast, then lard with strips of fat. Put the birds in a roasting tin, and cook for 10 minutes at 400°F (Mark 6) to seal in the juices. Sprinkle with salt and both peppers. Reduce heat to 350°F (Mark 4). Continue roasting for 20 to 30 minutes (depending upon the birds' age). When cooked, cut into portions and put in a pie dish. Add the butter to the dripping from the tin, season and pour over the birds. Leave until cold before eating.

※ ※ ※

There were other favourite dishes made from the free food of the countryside, such as Rook Pie and Pigeon Pie. Pigeon pie is still enjoyed and when I went out to Africa later on, living in the bush for months on end, I found that it came in very useful as an alternative to tinned corned beef.

PIGEON PIE

3 pigeons	*small pieces of ham, uncooked*
salt and pepper	*4 hard-boiled eggs, sliced*
butter	*stock*
2in squares of steak (about 8oz)	*1lb puff pastry*

Clean the pigeons, rub with salt and pepper, dusting inside the birds as well as outside, and put a small piece of butter inside each one. Line a pie dish with the steak, place the pigeons on top, then a piece of ham on each bird. Add the sliced hard-boiled eggs, half fill the dish with stock and cover with the pastry. Bake for 1½ hours in a hot oven, covering the pastry with wet greaseproof paper when browned.

(My steak in Africa had to be the tinned variety, but at least the pigeons helped the flavour!)

ROOK PIE

This was a Dales recipe and was traditionally eaten during the second week in May. Stew the breasts and legs of the birds gently, adding a small amount of steak and a tablespoon of good beef dripping. When cool, remove any bones and put the meat into a pie dish. Season well with salt and cayenne pepper, add a little of the juices and cover with shortcrust pastry. Bake in a hot oven until brown. Allow 1 rook per person.

＊　＊　＊

Besides the famous Yorkshire Pudding, there are many other traditional 'puddings' not used for a real pudding after the meal, but eaten as part of the main course. The first is really a variation on the 'Yorkshire'.

YORKSHIRE SAVOURY PUDDING

3oz flour
¾oz chopped sage
1 egg, lightly beaten
8oz white breadcrumbs

¾lb onions, chopped and boiled
½ pint milk
salt and pepper

Mix all to a fairly stiff consistency. Spoon into a greased pudding basin, cover with greaseproof paper and bake in a hot oven for 30 minutes. Serve with the main course.

SAVOURY PUDDING

1lb onions, finely chopped
6 tablespoons flour
salt and pepper
2 eggs
1 cup milk

2 tablespoons sage
2oz suet
4 tablespoons breadcrumbs
1 teaspoon baking powder
dripping

Boil the onions. Make a good stiff Yorkshire Pudding batter (see p27), add the onions, sage, suet, breadcrumbs and baking powder. Cook in very hot fat for about an hour.

❊   ❊   ❊

In the Calder Valley of the West Riding, near Hebden Bridge, the famous Dock Pudding was a traditional dish in early June, when the dock leaves were young and tender, and the nettles freshly green. Snakeweed—sometimes called bistort—is a small water dock with pink flowers, which grows in damp places.

This was also a very good remedy for those spring pimples and spots. My own family cure for them was a nauseatingly throat-gagging mixture of what was called brimstone and treacle, which consisted of large spoonfuls of flowers of sulphur mixed with black treacle; the memory of it remains. Spring in our household was something to be avoided at all costs—unless you were lucky enough to escape spots, and even then, the revolting mess was administered as a good old 'spring clean' of the system!

DOCK PUDDING

1 quart of snakeweed leaves *1 handful oatmeal*
1 pint young nettle tops *small knob of butter*
4 spring onions, finely chopped *bacon fat*

Clean and remove the thick stalks from the docks and nettles, and boil with the onions in a little water until tender. Add some seasoning and sprinkle in the oatmeal. Boil again for 10 minutes, stirring all the time. Add the butter. Leave overnight. Next day, fry large spoonfuls of the mixture in hot bacon fat and serve with bacon.

❈ ❈ ❈

Another wild plant, sorrel, was much used in late spring, and is still picked and used in France.

SORREL SOUP

Good handful sorrel leaves *3 large potatoes, finely chopped*
1oz butter *salt and pepper*
1 large onion, finely chopped *stock or water*

Wash the sorrel leaves, strip out and discard the stalks, then chop the remainder. Melt the butter, add the onion and cook gently for a few minutes. Add the chopped sorrel leaves and potatoes. Cook all together for 5 minutes, stirring all the time. Season. Cover with stock or water, and simmer until tender. If liked, the soup can be sieved; if too thick, add more stock or a little milk.

❈ ❈ ❈

Nettles were also used, when young and tender, to make Nettle Porridge.

NETTLE PORRIDGE

Gather young nettles in spring, when 2in high. Wash well, put into boiling salted water (about 1 pint nettles to 1 pint water). Boil until tender. Take out the nettles, chop them finely, return to the pan and thicken with fine oatmeal. Add pepper and a lump of butter, and boil up. Usually eaten with oatcakes for supper.

* * *

Two more puddings of the savoury kind were firm favourites in the mill towns, although one of them was a traditional speciality of the North-East.

HERB PUDDING (eaten on Good Friday)

2 eggs
1 pint milk
salt and pepper

4oz suet, finely chopped
1 pint breadcrumbs
2 teaspoons chopped parsley

Whisk the eggs, put into a pan with the milk and seasoning. Bring slowly to the boil, stirring as the mixture thickens. Add the finely chopped suet, breadcrumbs and chopped parsley. Pour into a greased pie dish and bake in a hot oven until brown on top.

PEASE PUDDING (an accompaniment to roast pork)

1 pint large yellow split peas
salt and pepper

knob of butter
1 egg yolk

Wash and dry the peas, tie loosely in a cloth and put into warm water. Boil for 2 hours until tender. Turn out into a basin, then mash well with salt and pepper to taste, the butter and egg yolk. Make into a smooth mix, tie up again in the cloth and boil for another hour.

Finally, a Yorkshire variation of good old Steak and Kidney
Pud.

EAST RIDING PUDDING

8oz flour
4oz suet
1 teaspoon baking powder
salt
½lb streaky pork

1 small onion, finely chopped
sliced potatoes
sage
salt and pepper

Make a suet crust pastry with the flour, suet, baking powder
and salt. Line a basin with two-thirds of the pastry. Into the
basin put ½lb streaky pork, cut into strips, the finely chopped
onion and sliced potatoes in layers, adding a pinch of sage and
salt and pepper to each layer. Repeat the layers until the basin
is full. Add 2 tablespoons water. Put on the remaining pastry as
a lid, cover tightly with a cloth and boil for 8 hours.

3 Puddings, Possets And Flummery

Mother's cooking, although very good, did not contain many puddings. Perhaps the main meals she made were so filling in themselves that we did not need 'afters'. She tended to stick to old favourites like rice pudding and something my brother called 'frogspawn' pud! But she did make one firm delight.

APPLE YORKSHIRE PUDDING

Make Yorkshire Pudding batter (see p 27), pour into hot dripping, put sliced apples on top. Bake for 30 minutes and serve dredged with sugar.

✿ ✿ ✿

There was also the old stand-by of plain Yorkshire Pudding served not with gravy, but with jam or simply sprinkled with sugar. Pancakes too were often served with jam, rolled up and oozing deliciously at the ends.

Most puddings eaten in Yorkshire are the good solid ones of childhood. Bread was often the base upon which a pudding was built, using up left-overs or otherwise, and always cheap and filling.

WHITE POT PUDDING

thin slices of white bread
thinly sliced apples
chopped suet
currants and raisins

sugar
1 nutmeg, grated
4 eggs, beaten
1 pint milk

Put a layer of bread in a greased dish, add a layer of apple, a layer of suet, some currants and raisins, and sprinkle with sugar and nutmeg. Repeat until the dish is full. Mix the beaten eggs with the milk, with more sugar and nutmeg to taste, then pour over the layers. Let it stand for 2 hours before baking in a medium oven for 30 minutes.

* * *

Teacakes were a great part of life in Yorkshire, round flat cakes, of plain or fruited bread, and what was not used up by toasting was used to make puddings.

TEACAKE PUDDING

1 teacake, fruited preferably
butter
3oz citron peel

3 eggs
½ pint milk
sugar, to taste

Cut the teacake into slices, buttering each slice. Place in a buttered basin, with peel between each slice. Beat the eggs, milk and sugar together and pour over the bread. Cover the basin and boil for 1 hour.

* * *

Yorkshire is not a county of orchards, the climate is against that, but we do manage to grow apples, and of course rhubarb. The area around Morley and Leeds was once one of the great rhubarb-growing districts, and in late spring field upon field would be full of the big-leaved plants, and encircled by canning factories. The result was that rhubarb was used in a good number of puddings.

44

This is the West Riding version of the classic Summer Pudding.

BREAD AND FRUIT PUDDING

Line a pudding bowl with crustless slices of bread. Fit the slices as closely together as possible. Drain hot stewed rhubarb and fill the basin with the fruit. Top with more closely fitting slices of bread. Put a weighted saucer on top and leave until cold. Then turn out and serve with cold custard.

BOILED RHUBARB PUDDING

12oz suet pastry   *4oz soft brown sugar*
5 sticks rhubarb

Line a buttered basin with two-thirds of the pastry. Cut the rhubarb into 1in lengths and fill the basin, adding the sugar. Cover with the remaining pastry. Pinch the edges tightly together, cover with a floured cloth, and boil for about 2 hours. Serve with sifted sugar and cream.

RHUBARB PUDDING

8oz shortcrust pastry   *½ cup soft brown sugar*
3 cups chopped rhubarb   *2 eggs, beaten*
3 tablespoons flour   *3 tablespoons thick cream*

Line an 8in pie plate with the pastry. Put in the chopped rhubarb. Mix the flour, sugar, eggs and cream, and cover the rhubarb with the mixture. Bake in a fairly hot oven for 10 minutes, then lower the heat and bake for a further 25 minutes, until the topping is set.

RHUBARB FRITTERS

Cut young rhubarb into 3in lengths, dip in batter and fry in deep fat. When golden brown, lift out, drain and sprinkle with sugar. Serve with cream.

❊ ❊ ❊

Another fritter recipe, this time using the other fruit stand-by, was Yorkshire Fritters.

YORKSHIRE FRITTERS

1lb plain flour
2 teaspoons salt
½ tablespoon sugar
2oz butter
1 egg, beaten
½oz fresh yeast

4 tablespoons milk and water
3oz currants
3oz raisins
4oz grated apple
caster sugar
5fl oz sherry

Sift the flour, salt and sugar together, rub in the butter. Mix in the beaten egg and the yeast dissolved in the milk and water. Knead, leave to rise, knock back. Work in the currants, raisins and apple. Divide into 24 round balls. Leave to prove, then deep fry in oil until golden brown. Drain, toss in caster sugar, sprinkle with warmed sherry and serve at once.

YORKSHIRE HONEY PUDDING

4oz butter
4oz sugar
2 eggs, beaten
4oz plain flour
pinch of salt

2oz soft brown sugar
½lb peeled, chopped apples
grated nutmeg
4oz honey

Cream the butter and sugar until fluffy, beat in the eggs, then fold in the flour and salt. Sprinkle the brown sugar in a 2½ pint greased pudding basin, put in the apples, nutmeg and honey, and pour the creamed mixture over. Cover and steam for about 2 hours. Serve with custard.

* * *

HANNAH MORE'S PUDDING
(an old recipe from the richer farming communities!)

6oz suet
6oz grated bread
6oz raisins
6oz sugar
3oz candied peel

½ nutmeg, grated
6oz minced apple
6 eggs
1 glass brandy

Mix the suet, bread, raisins, sugar, peel, nutmeg and apple. Beat the eggs well, add the brandy and stir well. Add to the other ingredients. Put into a greased basin, cover closely. Boil for 3 hours.

This pudding is better if mixed the day before boiling.

ELIZABETH RAFFALD'S APPLE PUDDING
(an eighteenth-century recipe)

shortcrust pastry to line a 7in
 flan tin
4oz stewed apples
4oz butter

3 eggs
3oz soft brown sugar
grated rind of 1 lemon

Line the flan tin with the pastry and bake blind. Cream the butter, add to the apples. Beat well. Beat the eggs with the sugar, add to the apple mixture, then add the grated lemon rind. Pour into the cooked pastry case and bake in a moderate oven for 30 minutes.

ALBERT'S PUDDING

6 eggs
6 apples, finely chopped
4oz sugar
6oz raisins

6oz fine breadcrumbs
a little grated nutmeg
pinch of salt

Beat the eggs well and add the rest of the ingredients. Mix well, put into a greased basin, cover and boil for 3 hours. Serve with sweet white sauce.

EGG AND APPLE PUDDING

1 egg
3oz sugar
½ pint milk

7 tablespoons flour
½ teaspoon salt
3 apples, peeled and chopped

Beat the egg with the sugar. Add the milk, flour and salt, mix
well. Stir in the apples. Put into a greased basin, cover, and boil
for 1½ hours. Serve with custard.

OLD-FASHIONED APPLE CHARLOTTE

slices of bread
3oz butter, melted
3lb apples
3oz butter

12oz sugar
juice of 1 lemon
½ teaspoon cinnamon

Butter a round cake tin. Line it with thin slices of bread dipped
in the melted butter, making sure that the slices overlap. Peel,
core and quarter the apples. Stew gently with the other 3oz
butter, the sugar, lemon juice and cinnamon, stirring frequently.
When cooked to a smooth, dry pulp, allow to cool, then put
into the tin, filling it to the top. Cover with more bread slices
dipped in butter, put a tin plate on the top and bake in a hot
oven for 45 minutes.

BROWN BETTY
(a variation on the previous recipe)

thin slices of apple
breadcrumbs
sugar

butter
cinnamon

In a greased basin, layer the apples, breadcrumbs and sugar,
putting a small piece of butter and a little cinnamon between
each layer. Sprinkle a very small amount of water over each
layer. Fill up the basin, making the top layer apple. Bake in a
hot oven and serve with cream.

* * *

My Auntie Kate would make a superb variation on the Summer Pudding (p45) as a rare treat whenever I went to stay with her in school holidays. She lived in a district of Ilkley known as Ben Rhydding, but I wonder if she had taken the recipe from the Scottish Ben Rhydding, since raspberries are very much a Scottish fruit? Anyway, we all benefited by it!

BEN RHYDDING PUDDING

2lb raspberries
sugar to taste
2 round sponge cakes
¾ pint milk

5fl oz thick cream
8 egg yolks
3oz sugar
5fl oz whipped cream

Simmer the fruit to a pulp and sweeten. Cut a round of sponge cake to fit the top of a 2½ pint mould. Cut the rest into thin slices and use to line the base and sides of the mould. Fill the basin with fruit and any left-over cake, cover with the sponge round. Set a weighted plate on top, then leave until the cake is soaked with fruit juice and cold. Make a rich custard sauce with the milk, cream, egg yolks and sugar. Leave to cool, then fold in the whipped cream. Turn out the fruit mould and pour the custard sauce over.

Needless to say, after that delight, a good stiff walk on Ilkley's famous Rombald's Moor was called for! And another good excuse for a walk was Yorkshire Sack Pudding.

YORKSHIRE SACK PUDDING
(which is nicer than it sounds!)

1 pint sherry (for starters!)
¼ teaspoon ground cinnamon
grated rind of 1 lemon
4oz sponge cake crumbs
6 eggs

orange-flower water
pinch of salt
1oz sugar
1oz butter
1oz currants

Beat the sherry, cinnamon, lemon rind and cake crumbs together. Leave to soak for 15 minutes. Beat the eggs, add a few drops of orange-flower water and the salt, then the sugar, butter and currants. Add the sherry mixture. Pour into a buttered 2½ pint dish and stand in a tin of hot water. Bake at 350°F (Mark 4) until set.

*   *   *

But there were also the everyday puddings, such as Rice and Raisin Pudding.

AUNTIE KATE'S RICE AND RAISIN PUDDING

½ cup pudding rice
½ cup golden syrup
½ cup raisins
½ teaspoon ground cinnamon

½ teaspoon salt
4 cups milk
1 teaspoon butter

Mix the rice with the syrup, raisins, cinnamon, salt and milk. Turn into a buttered pie dish. Bake in a slow oven for 2½ hours. Stir every 20 minutes for the first hour, then add the butter and leave to bake.

*   *   *

Another very old recipe is Carrot Pudding, odd-sounding but nice.

CARROT PUDDING

4 carrots, boiled and mashed
3 tablespoons breadcrumbs
6 eggs, beaten
small pinch of grated nutmeg
8oz butter

2 tablespoons rose water
1 tablespoon shredded lemon
  peel
6oz puff pastry

Mix all the ingredients together, put into a greased dish, cover with a puff pastry lid and bake in a hot oven.

SUET PUDDING

8oz flour
½ teaspoon salt

½ teaspoon baking powder
4oz suet, finely shredded

Mix the flour, salt, baking powder and suet to a stiff dough with water. Form into a long roll, wrap in a floured cloth, tie firmly. Cover with boiling water and boil for 1½ hours. Serve with jam, treacle or fruit.

* * *

And still on the sturdy puddings, a recipe for Currant Dumplings.

CURRANT DUMPLINGS

8oz flour
3oz suet
½ teaspoon salt

3oz currants
1 teaspoon baking powder
milk or water

Mix all to a firm dough with milk or water. Make into small dumplings, drop into boiling water and boil for 20 minutes, covered. Serve with custard.

* * *

51

UPPEY PUDDING

3oz dripping	*1 heaped teaspoon baking*
8oz flour	*powder*
1 tablespoon brown sugar	*milk to mix*

Rub the fat into the flour, then add the sugar and baking powder. Bind with milk to make a 'rocky' mixture. Shape into a long thin roll, like an elongated rock cake. Bake in a hot oven for 20 minutes. It should double in size and brown well. Serve with jam.

WEST RIDING PUDDING

4oz shortcrust pastry	*2 eggs*
a little jam	*4oz flour*
4oz butter	*½ teaspoon baking powder*
4oz sugar	

Line the sides of a pie dish with thinly rolled pastry, and spread with jam. Beat the butter and sugar, add the eggs, then stir in the flour and baking powder. Pour into the pie dish and bake at 350°F (Mark 4) for 1 hour.

RAILWAY PUDDING

6oz flour	*1 egg*
1 teaspoon baking powder	*milk to mix*
3oz butter	*jam*
3oz sugar	*a few drops of vanilla essence*

Sieve the flour and baking powder, rub in the fat, add the sugar. Beat the egg with a little milk, add to the other ingredients and mix to a soft consistency. Pour into a Yorkshire pudding tin and bake in a moderate oven. When just firm and golden, turn out, then split and spread with warmed jam. Put the pieces together, cut into squares and serve with custard.

* * *

TOFFEE PUDDING

10oz self-raising flour
1½oz suet
1½oz lard

water
3oz butter
2oz sugar

Make a shortcrust pastry with the flour, suet, lard and water. Roll out into an oblong. Cream the butter and sugar, and spread over the pastry. Roll up and close each end securely. Put into a pie dish and bake in a hot oven for 35 minutes. As the butter and sugar ooze out of the pastry, use this to baste the roll—it will form a toffee-like coating.

* * *

Batley was the town next door to my own—Dewsbury—in the West Riding, very similar in appearance, dirty and smoke-blackened. Indeed it was hard to tell where one town ended and the other began. There was great rivalry between them, though, and the rugby games fought were hard and bloody!

BATLEY PUDDING
(there doesn't seem to be a Dewsbury Pudding!)

3 egg yolks and 1 white
3oz caster sugar
15 almonds, blanched and
* pounded*

1 tablespoon brandy
2oz ground rice
½ pint thin cream
2oz clarified butter

Beat the egg yolks and white well, mix in the sugar. Add the almonds and brandy. Meanwhile, boil the ground rice with the cream. Let it cool, then stir in the butter and mix with the egg mixture. Bake in a moderate oven for 30 minutes.

* * *

Two very economical puddings now.

OATMEAL HASTY PUDDING

½ pint milk

1 dessertspoon oatmeal

1 dessertspoon flour

½ cup cold milk

Boil the ½ pint of milk with the oatmeal and a good pinch of salt. Mix the flour with the ½ cup of cold milk and add to the boiling mixture. Stir until it thickens, then cook for about 20 minutes. Add jam to serve.

PORRIDGE PUDDING

Put left-over porridge into small greased cups or moulds. When set, turn out and surround with cooked prunes. Add some whipped cream.

* * *

And to end the puddings, a lovely old one that unfortunately cannot be made, as the cowslip is a protected plant.

COWSLIP PUDDING

1 pint cowslip petals

½ pint milk

2oz breadcrumbs

2oz sugar

1oz butter

3 egg yolks

1 dessertspoon lemon juice

Stew the petals in the milk until tender, then add the other ingredients. Steam in a buttered mould for 1½ hours. Serve with Cowslip Sauce.

COWSLIP SAUCE

3 egg whites

1 cup cowslip wine

1oz sugar

Beat the egg whites. Add the wine and sugar, and beat over heat to a thick froth.

Yorkshire is not always the dour, cold place that it is described as, and in summertime, when the fells are green, dotted with the white-coated hardy sheep and criss-crossed by the ancient stone walls, it can be a gentle land, smelling of wild thyme and heather with white limestone scars gleaming under a blue sky. Walking across a heather-covered hill then is a wonderful experience, with the sad curlew singing his plaintive song, and grouse whirring suddenly from under one's feet. Even the high giants—Penyghent, a crouching lion-shaped mountain, and mighty Ingleborough with its gritstone capping—can be benevolent, although the winds still blow chilly up there, on the top of Yorkshire.

It is a different land from the one I grew up with, no smoke or sooty grit, clear skies and clean air; and I remember with gratitude those first days on the moors above Ilkley, when my uncle would walk me for miles, 'to get the soot out of you' he would say. Along past the small tarn, across to the huge rocks called the Cow and Calf, scratched and scored by generations of learner climbers out from Leeds and Bradford; and down through Rocky Valley with its mysterious, ancient Swastika Stone, which gained a new meaning for me in later years. From my uncle, who was a quiet, gentle man, a shoemaker by trade, I learned how to enjoy the hills, and I have never forgotten.

In the warm days of summer even our sturdy Yorkshire appetites would seek food that was a little lighter, if only the puddings, and we tasted delights that had come down through the farming ages to soothe a hot and dusty throat. The most famous one was syllabub, of course, and this was not just a local recipe—any farming community had learned how to make use of new milk in any age or place. But for sheer simplicity, it has never been beaten.

To be properly made, syllabub should be milk drawn straight from the cow into wine, and then flavoured to taste with cinnamon or lemon. And because of the suddenness of the mixing, the name became synonymous with frothiness. Charlotte Brontë, in *Shirley*, writes of 'whipping up a syllabub sonnet'. For those of us without a cow at the back door, here is a more modern recipe!

55

SYLLABUB

1 pint thin cream
3 egg whites
3 tablespoons wine

grated rind and juice of 1 lemon
sugar to taste
brandy

Whisk together the cream, egg whites, wine, lemon rind and juice, and sugar. Put some brandy into glasses, and as the froth rises on the whipped mixture, fill up the brandy glasses with it.

WHIPPED SYLLABUB

2 small bowls thin cream
1 small bowl white wine
grated rind of 1 lemon

3 egg whites
sugar

Mix the cream, wine and lemon rind. Whip the egg whites to a froth, sweeten to taste, then add to the cream and wine.

LEMON POSSET

1 pint thick cream
½ pint white wine, slightly
    sweetened

grated rind and juice of 2
    lemons
2 egg whites

Mix the cream and the wine, then add the lemon rind and juice. Whisk the egg whites to a froth and then add them to the wine mixture.

FLUMMERY

grated rind and juice of 3
    lemons
½ pint boiling water
8oz white sugar

¼oz gelatine, dissolved in 3
    tablespoons hot water
4 egg yolks
sherry

Add the grated lemon rind to the boiling water and sugar, and leave to stand for 30 minutes. Strain the dissolved gelatine into this mixture, add the lemon juice and egg yolks. Put the mixture into a jug, then stand the jug in a pan of boiling water.

Stir gently over a low heat until the mixture thickens like custard, being careful not to overheat. Strain, and when cool, add a glass of sherry. Serve in tall glasses.

CLOUTED CREAM

4 blades mace
½ pint fresh milk
6 teaspoons rose water

2 egg yolks, well beaten
1 quart thin cream

Put the mace into the milk with the rose water. Simmer for a few minutes. Gradually stir in the beaten egg yolks. Mix in the cream and stir over heat until hot, but do not boil. Pour into a deep dish and allow to stand for 24 hours. Eat with fruit.

❅ ❅ ❅

If Heathcliff had tasted this, he might not have been so surly!

HAWORTH CREAM

3 eggs, separated
½lb caster sugar
grated rind and juice of 2
    lemons

4 teaspoons gelatine, dissolved
    in a glass of hot water

Mix the egg yolks and sugar, add the lemon rind and juice, and the hot gelatine solution. Pour into a dish. Whip the egg whites stiffly and fold into the mixture. When set, top with whipped cream.

Who can blame Heathcliff though, living in such a wild spot? The moors around Haworth are truly wild—dark and heather-covered, often gloomy with shadows, scarcely ever bright. There is another side to Yorkshire there, the grim determination to hang on whatever happens, and it shows in the black gritstone outcrops and lonely tracks that disappear over the far edges of the hills.

❅ ❅ ❅

On the other side of the county a different picture emerges. The great green plain of York with its gentle background of the Hambledon Hills, and the softly rolling contours of the moors that reach the sea, are far removed from the scowling face of Heathcliff's domain. York itself, dominated by its storybook cathedral, is a wonder of medieval streets and modern architecture, and odd patches of slum clearance; and even the air there is more gentle. Down from the rugged Pennines, the weather has been tempered by the time it reaches that great plain, and the driving rain of the fells is used up long before it crosses the flat grassland to York, so that the following recipe is aptly named for a gentle place.

YORK VELVET

4 or 5 large apples, peeled
   cored and sliced
apricot jam
1oz arrowroot
1 pint cold milk

1 pint cold milk
½oz butter
sugar to taste
browned breadcrumbs

Put the apples into a greased dish and spread with apricot jam. Mix the arrowroot into the cold milk, with the butter, and sweeten to taste. Stir over heat until it boils, then pour slowly onto the apples and jam. Sprinkle breadcrumbs on top, and bake until golden brown.

❋ ❋ ❋

And another recipe from York is York Soufflé.

YORK SOUFFLÉ

½lb puff pastry
5 eggs
½lb caster sugar

grated rind and juice of 2
   lemons
2 oz butter

Line a dish with puff pastry. Beat the eggs, stir in the sugar and the lemon rind and juice. Melt the butter and pour into the mixture. Put into the dish and bake until risen.

❋ ❋ ❋

And finally, from the rhubarb fields of the West Riding, comes Rhubarb Cream.

RHUBARB CREAM

12 stalks of rhubarb	*½in piece cinnamon*
grated rind and juice of 1 lemon	*1¼ cups caster sugar*
3 cloves	*1¼ cups whipped cream*

Peel the rhubarb, cut it into 1in lengths and put into a pan. Add the juice and grated rind of the lemon, the cloves and cinnamon. Cover and cook gently until the juice runs freely, then add the sugar and continue cooking until it is smooth and dry, taking care not to let it burn. Cool, then remove the cloves. Fold in the cream and serve in tall glasses, decorated with whipped cream.

The glorious pudding of Yorkshire may be king, but the pie is the queen. Pastry making is an art made glorious 'by this sun of York'—as Shakespeare might have said. The fruit pies and tarts of the Broad Acres are renowned, and their decoration has been brought to a fine art. There are traditional embellishments to the various open tarts and pies, and woe betide anyone who puts the wrong lattice weave on top of her treacle tart.

The most famous pie is a savoury one, the Stand Pie, already described, but there is an older one still, too rich for today's taste perhaps, but worthy of a place in Yorkshire's gastronomic history.

YORKSHIRE CHRISTMAS PIE
(an eighteenth-century recipe)

Take a goose, chicken, partridge, turkey and pigeon, and open each down the back. Bone them and flatten them out. Season all well with a mixture of $\frac{1}{2}$oz each mace, black pepper and nutmeg, $\frac{1}{4}$oz ground cloves and 2 heaped teaspoons salt.

Place each bird, beginning with the smallest, into the next in size, finishing with the turkey, so that it looks like one enormous bird. Truss and put into a raised pie crust; fill up any spaces with chopped-up hare or woodcock, and forcemeat. Put 2lb butter on top, cover with a lid of pastry and bake for 4 hours.

Another very early pie was the Egg Pie, similar to mince pies, but probably of earlier origins.

EGG PIE FILLING

6 hard-boiled eggs *1lb currants*
6 apples, finely chopped *sugar, mace and nutmeg to taste*
1lb suet *2 tablespoons brandy*

Rub the eggs through a sieve, mix with the apples, suet and currants. Season with sugar, mace and nutmeg, and add the brandy. Use as mincemeat in pies.

❋ ❋ ❋

It was traditional in Yorkshire, a long time ago, to make the mince pies in an oval shape, representing the manger of the infant Jesus. It was a test of orthodoxy: if a visitor ate an oval pie, it was a sign that he was a true Christian! And the pies were to be eaten only for the twelve days, beginning on Christmas Day, at the rate of one per person per day, thus ensuring twelve happy months to come.

There are other pies with historical backgrounds, such as the Wilfra Week Pie from Ripon. This was eaten at the August Bank Holiday, which coincided with the feast of St Wilfred, the patron saint of Ripon Cathedral. At the same time, all the housewives would also make Wilfra Tarts, which were jam and lemon curd tarts. These were then piled on plates just inside the doorways of the houses and passing people were invited to take them.

WILFRA WEEK PIE

6oz shortcrust pastry *golden syrup*
thinly sliced apples *grated cheese*

Line a swiss roll tin with shortcrust pastry. Cover with a layer of thinly sliced apples, about ¾in thick. Cover with golden syrup and a sprinkling of grated cheese. Cover with a pastry lid and bake in a moderate oven for 30 minutes.

Another pie with a foot in history is Stamford Bridge Spear Pie, made to commemorate the famous battle of Stamford Bridge, when Harold and his men beat the invading Norsemen, in September 1066. The story goes that the Norsemen were being driven back, but one lone soldier was holding the bridge and thus preventing the final triumph of the English. An English soldier went underneath the old bridge in a coracle, and by thrusting his spear up through the wooden planking managed to kill the lone Norseman. The pies to celebrate this somewhat gruesome victory are made in the shape of small boats, filled with a whole spiced pear; the stalk of the pear is left standing upright to signify the spear!

Also commemorating St Wilfred of Ripon are Wilfra Cheese-cakes.

WILFRA CHEESECAKES

8oz shortcrust pastry   *2oz ground almonds*
½ pint milk   *1oz caster sugar*
1oz white breadcrumbs   *grated rind of 1 lemon*
4oz butter   *3 eggs*

Line 16 tartlet tins with the pastry. Boil the milk, stir in the breadcrumbs. Leave for 10 minutes, then add the butter, ground almonds, sugar and lemon rind. Beat in the eggs, one at a time. Pour mixture into the tartlet tins and bake at 350°F (Mark 4) until set.

* * *

The cheesecake of Yorkshire is a splendid creation in its own right. However, an older recipe known as a curd tart also has strong affinities with the sturdy cheesecakes of Europe. In Yorkshire it is made in saucers, on a shortcrust base.

YORKSHIRE CURD TARTS

8oz rich shortcrust pastry   *2oz currants*
8oz curds   *2 eggs, beaten*
4oz caster sugar   *ground nutmeg*

62

Line 4 saucers with the pastry. Mix the curds with the sugar, currants and beaten eggs. Spoon on to the saucers, sprinkle with nutmeg and bake until golden brown.

Sometimes a little lemon rind, or candied peel, may be added, but the above recipe is the more usual one.

*　*　*

Another tart or pie for which Yorkshire is famous is the custard tart, a small, deep, open tart filled with a golden set custard. It is sold everywhere throughout Yorkshire and is asked for simply by the name 'custards'.

YORKSHIRE CUSTARDS

8oz rich shortcrust pastry　　*1½oz caster sugar*
½ pint milk　　*grated nutmeg*
3 egg yolks

Line deep, individual pie tins with the pastry. Heat the milk to blood temperature. Beat the egg yolks and sugar together, then pour the milk in, still beating. Strain into the tart tins and sprinkle with nutmeg. Bake at 400°F (Mark 6) for 30 minutes, then at 350°F (Mark 4) for about 15 minutes, until a knife blade inserted in the centre comes out clean.

*　*　*

Treacle is another love of the Yorkshireman, and, like the Scot, he has many favourite dishes which include treacle, black or golden. One of the best loved is the tart filled with treacle.

YORKSHIRE TREACLE TART

8oz shortcrust pastry　　*golden syrup*
1oz fine breadcrumbs　　*1oz butter*

Line a plate with the pastry. Sprinkle half the crumbs on to it, then add a layer of syrup and top with the rest of the crumbs. The tart should not be more than half filled. Dot with small pieces of butter. Using scraps left over from the pastry, make a woven lattice over the filling. Bake in a hot oven until golden.

Apple pie is a favourite with the men, but the true Yorkshire way of eating it is somewhat different. It must always be offered with a good thick chunk of the beloved Wensleydale cheese. To a Yorkshireman, apple pie without cheese is like a kiss without a squeeze, and for the true fanatic, the cheese can even be baked in with the apple!

YORKSHIRE APPLE TARTLETS

6oz plain flour
3oz lard
½ teaspoon salt
2 tablespoons milk
apples, peeled and finely
  chopped

ground cloves
honey
grated cheese

Make shortcrust pastry with the flour, lard, salt and milk. Roll out thinly into 9 circles to fit tart tins, with 9 extra circles for lids. Fill the tart cases with chopped apple, then sprinkle ground cloves over to taste. Add 1 teaspoon thin honey to each. Cover with grated cheese. Put on the pastry lids, seal well and snip small steam holes. Bake at 400°F (Mark 6) for about 25 minutes.

RHUBARB PIE

A traditional fruit pie in the West Riding, made with rich shortcrust pastry and slightly tart rhubarb.

Line a pie plate with pastry, fill with short pieces of rhubarb, then sprinkle liberally with a mixture of sugar and cornflour. Top with a pastry lid and bake until golden brown. While still hot, sprinkle with caster sugar.

* * *

Bilberries, those tiny purply-blue berries of the heather moors, form the fruit filling for another great Yorkshire favourite. The Americans call them blueberries, the Scots call them blaeberries, but the rich purple juice is the same everywhere, making a memorable pie.

When I stayed at Ilkley, there were many forages on to the moors in August and September to pick bilberries. It is a finicky job, as the fruit is so tiny and easily squashed, and the deep blue stains the fingers, but once the richly smelling pie comes out of the oven, all the back-breaking labour is forgotten.

YORKSHIRE BILBERRY PIE

1½lb bilberries	8oz puff pastry
4 cooking apples	2 tablespoons thick cream
8oz sugar	1 egg white, beaten

Bake the apples and scrape out the pulp. Mix it with the bilberries and sugar. Line a pie plate with pastry, fill with fruit and sugar, and cover with pastry. Do not seal. Brush the top with beaten egg white, sprinkle with sugar and bake in a hot oven until golden brown. Gently lift the lid and pour in very thick cream.

* * *

Pastry is used to make many other traditional goodies too. The most famous is the Fat Rascal, which has developed from using up left-over pastry, making it into a cake in its own right.

The first version was simple enough. Scraps of shortcrust pastry left from baking were rolled out, sprinkled with sugar and a few currants, rolled up again and made into a flat cake. This was baked, then eaten hot, spread with butter.

YORKSHIRE FAT RASCALS (the true version)

8oz plain flour	1oz light brown sugar
¼ teaspoon salt	3 tablespoons milk
4oz butter	caster sugar
2oz currants	

Sift flour and salt, rub in the butter. Add the currants and sugar. Stir in the milk and about 1 tablespoon water. Mix to a firm dough. Knead lightly and roll to ½in thickness. Cut into 2in rounds. Place on a greased baking tray, then dredge tops with caster sugar. Bake in a fairly hot oven for about 20 minutes.

65

YORKSHIRE MINT PASTY

12oz shortcrust pastry
2oz currants
2oz raisins
1oz peel
1½oz brown sugar
pinch of mixed spice

1 tablespoon fresh mint,
   chopped
1½oz butter
milk
caster sugar

Roll out the pastry ¼in thick, cut into 8 rounds. Mix fruit, brown sugar, spice and chopped mint; bind with butter. Put onto the pastry rounds, fold over and seal. Brush with milk, sprinkle with caster sugar and bake in a hot oven until golden brown.

* * *

Another sort of pasty, marvellous for a winter day on the fells.

RUM PASTY

8oz currants
8oz shortcrust pastry
sugar

butter
rum
milk

Cover the currants with cold water, bring slowly to the boil. When soft, drain and dry. Cover a tart plate with thinly rolled shortcrust pastry, then spread the currants over. Dust with sugar. Dot with butter, sprinkle liberally with rum, cover with pastry and seal the edges. Brush with milk and bake in a hot oven.

MOGGY

This rather peculiar name has nothing to do with cats! It probably derives from the Norse name for corn—*mugi*. In early English too, corn was called *muga* or *muge*.

1½lb flour
½ teaspoon salt
3 teaspoons baking powder
6oz lard

6oz butter
8oz sugar
8oz golden syrup
milk

Sift the flour, salt and baking powder, rub in the fats. Add the sugar and syrup, then mix to a stiff dough with the milk. Cut into 2 pieces, roll out to $\frac{1}{2}$in thick and bake in a moderate oven until pale brown. Cut into squares before cooling.

MATRIMONY CAKE

shortcrust pastry　　　　*chopped mixed peel*
currants　　　　　　　　 *butter*
sugar　　　　　　　　　　*milk*

Line a baking plate with shortcrust pastry. Sprinkle freely with currants, sugar and peel, dab with butter. Place a round of pastry over, proceed as before. Cover with another pastry round, score with a knife. Brush with milk, sprinkle with sugar and bake in a hot oven until browned. When cold, cut into fingers.

YORKSHIRE GRIDDLE CAKES

1lb flour　　　　　　　　*1 teaspoon baking powder*
good pinch of salt　　　　*2oz milk or buttermilk*
2oz currants

Mix all together in a basin with enough milk to make a fairly stiff dough. Roll out into thin cakes, then bake quickly on a hot griddle until golden brown. Split the cakes open and butter whilst hot.

* * *

Like Ireland and Scotland, Yorkshire has a peat-cutting tradition known as 'turbary'. Everywhere on the fells, there are old tracks, worn by centuries of cart wheels, made by the local people going to exercise their rights of turbary, that is, the right to cut peats for their fires. And the fells still bear the signs of the cutting—large bare patches where the turf has been removed and is now slowly growing back. The ancient tracks make splendid ways for fell walkers.

YORKSHIRE TURF CAKES

1lb flour   *8oz butter*
1 teaspoon salt

Rub half the butter into the flour and salt, mix to a stiff dough with water. Roll out, dot with bits of butter, then fold and roll. Continue as for puff pastry, and finally cut into small rounds about ½in thick. Grease a deep frying pan and put in the cakes. Heap burning turves under and on top of the pan. Alternatively, bake in a hot oven. Bake until golden.

Finally, three recipes used in the Dales: one for pig-killing day and two for haymaking time.

MELL CAKES
(from the Danish or Icelandish *mel* or *mjol*—meal)

Pig-killing day was a day for a party, when all friends and nearby farmers would gather at the farmhouse. These cakes were traditionally served then.

Make some shortcrust pastry with added sugar and currants. Roll into flat cakes 9in across, ¾in thick. Bake until brown, then split open whilst hot, spread with butter and sprinkle with sugar and grated nutmeg. Sandwich together, spread the top with the same mix.

NODDEN CAKES

When haymaking was in progress, vast batches of this recipe were made and eaten—really nothing more than a good shortcrust pastry but more sustaining than bread.

Make a shortcrust pastry with 1lb flour, 8oz butter, salt and water. Roll out thinly, cut into squares. Bake as for pastry and eat well buttered.

SAD CAKES

Very similar to Nodden Cakes, but baked in one piece, then cut into rounds or squares which are often sandwiched with treacle.

5 Climb-a-Mountain Cakes

Until the outbreak of World War II, Yorkshire wives would bake their own bread, taking a pride in doing so; and on baking day, the warm rich smell of barm, as yeast is called in the North, would fill the farmhouses and the dingy little terraced houses alike. There would be big, golden loaves of bread baked in two-pound loaf tins, and the smaller oven-bottom cakes, and scores of other yeasty things.

OVEN-BOTTOM CAKE

$1\frac{1}{2}$*lb plain flour*
$\frac{1}{2}$ *tablespoon salt*
$\frac{1}{2}$*oz fresh yeast*

$\frac{1}{2}$ *tablespoon sugar*
$\frac{3}{4}$ *pint warm water*
4oz lard

Sift the flour and salt. Cream the yeast and sugar in a little of the water, add to the flour. Mix to a smooth dough with the rest of the water, knead, then leave to rise. Knock back when risen. Cut the lard into small pieces and stick them into the dough. With the knuckles, shape the dough into a cake, leaving it lumpy. Put on a greased baking sheet and leave to prove. When the dough has doubled in size, bake on the bottom of the oven at 425°F (Mark 7) for 10 minutes, then at 375°F (Mark 5) for 35 minutes.

A similar bread was called Shillie Cake.

SHILLIE CAKE

Take a good piece of bread dough. Roll out and spread with
small pieces of lard. Fold up, roll out again, spread with more
lard. Repeat twice more. Then bake on the bottom of the oven
at 350°F (Mark 4). When baked, split and spread with plenty of
butter. It is best eaten hot.

* * *

With the plain breads were baked slightly fancier ones, with
fruit added, although the next recipe, for Lardy Cake, was
traditionally made plain, and fruit was added only in more
recent times.

LARDY CAKE

Make 2lb bread dough. When it has risen, work in 8oz lard and
6oz sugar. If liked, currants can also be added. Shape into a
flattish round cake and bake in a fairly hot oven.

* * *

In Yorkshire, as in most of the North, teatime meant high tea, a
meal of heartening foods such as ham and eggs, scones, home-
made bread and jam, and toasted wonders such as Yorkshire
Teacakes and Pikelets. Pikelets are the Northern version of
crumpets, and are delicious toasted and eaten hot with butter
and treacle.

PIKELETS

½oz yeast   1¼lb flour
1 pint warm water   1oz salt

Cream the yeast in a little of the warm water. Sift the flour and
salt and stir in the remaining water. Add the creamed yeast to
the mix and cover with a cloth, leaving to rise. Thin the dough
to a thick batter with a little more warm water and leave for a

further 5 minutes. Grease some crumpet rings, and place on a hot griddle. Half fill with batter, and cook until dry on top. Turn the pikelets over, removing the rings. Holes will form in the batter as it cooks; if these do not form, the batter is too thick, and must be thinned with more warm water.

* * *

The Yorkshire Teacake comes in two varieties, plain or fruited; both are delicious when eaten fresh from the oven with lots of butter, and should any be left over, they are delicious toasted.

YORKSHIRE TEACAKES

1lb flour
1 teaspoon salt
1oz lard
1oz fresh yeast
1 teaspoon sugar

2oz currants and sultanas,
mixed
1oz sugar
½ pint warm milk

Sieve the flour and salt into a bowl, rub in the lard, put in a warm place. Cream the yeast and the teaspoon of sugar. Make a well in the flour with a wooden spoon, add the fruit and sugar, the creamed yeast and some of the milk. Draw the flour down into the well and gradually add more milk and flour to make a soft dough. Beat well until smooth. Cover the basin with a cloth and leave in a warm place to rise to the top of the bowl (about 1 hour).

Turn out when risen on to a floured board and knead. Divide into 6 pieces, kneading each, and roll out about ½in thick. Leave on a greased baking sheet to prove until double the height, and spongy. Bake in a hot oven for about 15 minutes.

* * *

The traditional bread of the Dales was Haver Bread, a name supposed to be Teutonic in origin, brought to England in the twelfth century. It is also called Skipton Oatcake, Ingleborough Riddle Bread and Clap Bread. The Riddle Bread is so called because of the holes in it, resembling a riddle (sieve), whilst the

Clap Bread owes its name to the clapping action as the long piece of oatcake was flung down along the table to stretch it thinly.

It was made in quantity in the Dales farms, and stored by hanging up on a creel suspended from the kitchen ceiling. These creels were later adapted into airing racks for the ironed washing! The bread was made like a thick batter and cooked on a bakston, or bakestone, a slate slab under which a fire was lit. Many old Dales farmhouses still have their bak-ston incorporated alongside the old kitchen fireplace. When the batter was mixed, the correct way to transfer it to the bakestone was by throwing it in a deft way so as to spread it out as thinly and evenly as possible.

It is a Spartan form of bread, but an admirable one for keeping or for taking up the steep sides of Ingleborough Mountain, or any of the great fells of Yorkshire; and the marvellous views from the tops are truly enhanced by the energy-giving oatcake. Alternatively, should the heavy mists catch you out, the oatcakes will sustain you as you tramp through the peat bogs and gulleys.

INGLEBOROUGH RIDDLE BREAD

Mix pinhead oatmeal and salt to a soft batter with cold water. If 'throwing' cannot be attempted, make into small balls then roll them out as thinly as possible on a greased, oatmeal-sprinkled surface. Bake on a hot bakestone or griddle, turning to bake both sides. Eat with butter and cheese.

* * *

High teas and holidays are the times of Yorkshire hospitality, and Christmas is one of the holidays when the tea tables groan with good things. At Christmas, any visitor is automatically offered Spice Cake and cheese, and it is shameful indeed to a Yorkshire housewife if she is caught with her cake tin empty.

My father had a sweet tooth, and there is the awful tale of the first Christmas that he and mother were married. She had proudly made her spice cakes a month in advance, so that they would improve with keeping, and a few days before Christmas, when friends called, she went to get one out. To her horror the tin was empty. It seemed that father, feeling peckish in the late evenings, had helped himself to spice cake, day after day, not realising until it was too late how much he had managed to eat. Mother had quite a ferocious temper, so I can imagine what sort of Christmas poor old father had that year!

In some parts of the county, this is called Yule Cake, but Spice Cake is the traditional West Riding name.

YORKSHIRE SPICE CAKE

4lb plain flour   *1½ lb soft brown sugar*
1 tablespoon salt   *1 teaspoon mixed spice*
8oz lard   *1 teaspoon grated nutmeg*
12oz butter   *3lb currants*
1½oz fresh yeast   *4 eggs, beaten*
1½ pints warm water

Sift the flour and salt, rub in the lard and butter. Cream the yeast with a little warm water, add it to the flour. Blend in the sugar and the rest of the water, then beat to a smooth dough. Knead well and leave to rise. When risen, knock back and work in the spices, currants and the beaten eggs. Knead again, divide the dough into 3, and put into 3 greased loaf tins. Leave in a warm place to prove, then bake at 400°F (Mark 6) for about 50 minutes.

*   *   *

More recipes that produced a cross between a bread and a cake, eaten at high tea, were those for Birstall Buns and the curiously named Wiggs.

BIRSTALL BUNS

1lb plain flour   *2oz butter*
2 teaspoons salt   *1 egg, beaten*
½oz fresh yeast   *3oz sultanas*
½ tablespoon sugar   *3oz currants*
4fl oz milk and water   *½oz chopped candied peel*

Sift the flour and salt. Cream the yeast and sugar. Warm the milk and water and butter until the butter is melted. Add the yeast mix and the beaten egg to the flour, then mix to a smooth dough with the milk and butter. Knead and leave to rise. Knock back when well risen, work in the fruits and knead again. Make into 12 round buns and leave on a greased baking sheet to prove. When doubled in size, bake at 425°F (Mark 7) for 12 minutes.

WIGGS

2 tablespoons fresh yeast
1 pint thin cream
1lb butter
2 eggs

2 egg yolks
2lb flour
8oz sugar
8oz caraway seeds

Cream the yeast with a little of the cream, mix with the butter, eggs, egg yolks, flour and the rest of the cream. Leave to rise. Add the sugar and caraway seeds, knead well and leave to prove in a greased square tin. When doubled in size, bake in a hot oven.

In Pateley Bridge, in the old West Riding, a traditional form of fritters was made and eaten on Fritter or Frutas Wednesday, during Shrovetide. They were sweet and fruity, and eaten hot.

PATELEY FRITTERS

¾oz fresh yeast
1 pint warm milk
12oz flour
1oz lard
pinch of cinnamon
pinch of salt
3oz currants

1½oz raisins
1 tablespoon sugar
2 tablespoons chopped lemon peel
1 large apple, chopped into small pieces

Crumble the yeast into a little of the warm milk, let it froth. Warm the flour. Melt the lard in the rest of the milk. Pour the yeast into a well in the centre of the flour, add the lard and milk, let it rise for a few minutes. Add the rest of the ingredients and beat to a stiff batter. Leave to rise for 1 hour in a warm place. Fry tablespoonfuls of the batter in dripping, turning when the underside is browned. Sprinkle with sugar and eat while hot.

There were other forms of bread, not made with yeast; the two common ones were Brompton Water Cakes and Brown Soda Bread. The Water Cakes were originally made by the Brompton weavers of Northallerton in the old North Riding, over a hundred years ago, and may possibly be a version of the old English *wafre* since they were made very thin. They were a very quick substitute for bread for the hardworking weavers. The Brown Soda Bread was often made midway through the week, when my mother's stocks were getting low, and she did not want to heat the oven too much. An even quicker 'filler' was Bakston Cake, a sort of shortbread-cum-scone, very good when eaten hot.

BROMPTON WATER CAKES

1lb plain flour
2 small teaspoons baking powder

½ teaspoon salt
water to mix

Mix all the ingredients to a firm dough. Roll out as thinly as possible into flat cakes and place on a greased baking sheet. Leave to rise for 5 minutes. Bake in a hot oven for 25 minutes.

BROWN SODA BREAD

2½ cups white flour
1 teaspoon salt
1 teaspoon bicarbonate of soda
2½ cups sour milk

2½ cups wholemeal flour
1 tablespoon melted butter
1¼ cups golden syrup

Brush 2 loaf tins with melted butter. Sift the white flour and salt into a basin. Dissolve the bicarbonate of soda in the sour milk. Add the wholemeal flour to the white flour; make a well in the centre, and add the sour milk, butter and syrup. Mix to a batter. Pour into the tins and bake in a slow oven for about 2 hours. Turn out and cool on a rack.

BAKSTON CAKE

2oz butter
1 cup flour

½ teaspoon salt
milk to mix

Rub the butter into the flour and salt, and mix to a fairly stiff dough with milk. Cut into 2 pieces and roll each to the size of a small tea plate. Bake on both sides, on a greased griddle (or frying pan). Split in half while still hot and butter well. This was an excellent after-school snack.

❊　❊　❊

Finally, another cross between a cake and a bread.

FRUIT AND NUT LOAF

2 eggs
their weight in sugar
their weight in flour
2oz stoned dates, chopped into small pieces
2oz mixed peel, chopped

2oz figs, chopped into small pieces
2oz walnuts, chopped
2oz hazelnuts, chopped
2oz almonds, shredded
grated rind and juice of 1 lemon

Butter an oblong cake tin. Separate the egg yolks and whites. Whisk the yolks and sugar until thick and creamy. Sieve the flour, then fold into the yolks and sugar. Whip the egg whites until stiff and fold into the flour mixture alternately with the rest of the ingredients. Turn the mixture into the tin and bake in a moderate oven until golden brown.

This is also very good cut into slices, toasted lightly, then rolled in icing sugar.

* * *

Perhaps because of the climate in Yorkshire, tea was always a 'sit-down' meal, something to be taken seriously, with none of the tiny cakes and cucumber sandwiches beloved of the novelist. Even a funeral was an occasion for a 'reight good tea', and a Yorkshire funeral was a miserable failure if no good York ham was offered, or 'a bit of tongue' and, naturally, all the many varieties of bread given in this chapter. A Yorkshireman lived well during his life, and he tried to make sure that his friends would give him a good send-off when he died, by leaving enough money to provide the 'sit-down tea'.

And indeed, on a cold winter's day, can there be anything more welcoming than a big brown teapot full of strong brew, and plates piled with hot pikelets and teacakes, butter oozing all over them? And after that, the rich, sweet, gingery and spicy cakes for which the Broad Acres are so famous.

6 Ginger, Spice And Treacle Delights

'Sugar and spice and all things nice . . .' it must surely have been a Yorkshireman who wrote that, for right through the range of Yorkshire cooking runs the rich smell of spice and dark treacle and it has left a splendid heritage of cakes and buns.

There is a wealth of recipes that include treacle in their ingredients, but none more famous surely than Yorkshire Parkin. This must never be overbaked or it will be dry and it must always be allowed to 'come again' in its tin before being eaten, allowing as long as possible between baking day and eating day, so that the result is a dark, crumbling stickiness that melts in the mouth. Once again, one of the main ingredients is oatmeal, the sturdy standby of the dales folk from way back in history, combined with sweet treacle. Oats were a staple commodity grown in the Dales, but how the tradition of treacle and syrup gained such a hold appears to be a mystery.

Lancashire has the same tradition of parkin, but its magic properties are sometimes completely lost on 'foreigners'. I remember how, when I was living under canvas in the East African bush, with my husband and one other surveyor in camp with us, I proudly made a tinful of parkin and gave some to bachelor George. Sadly I watched him chewing it and trying to appear pleased when it was apparent that he hated it. Brought up as I was on weekly parkin, I never could understand George.

There are many variations on the recipe for parkin, and every household has its own, treasured and handed down as the 'best'. It can also be made in small buns, which was the way in which it was sold in the shops for Bonfire Night—dark and sticky, sunken in the centre, and a strange new delight after mother's golden cake.

YORKSHIRE PARKIN I

4oz soft brown sugar	8oz plain flour
4oz butter	8oz medium oatmeal
8oz syrup	1 level teaspoon ground ginger
1 egg	½ teaspoon bicarbonate of soda
¼ pint milk	

Melt the sugar, butter and syrup over a low heat. Beat the egg well and add to the syrup mix with some of the milk. Sift the flour, oatmeal and ginger into a bowl and pour in the syrup mix. Dissolve the bicarbonate of soda in the remaining milk and add to the rest of the mix. Stir well, then pour into a greased tin, 11 by 9 by 2in. Bake until firm in a moderate oven (about 1 hour). Keep for about 1 week before eating.

YORKSHIRE PARKIN 2

8oz flour	4oz butter
4oz oatmeal	4oz dark treacle
6oz brown sugar	milk to mix
1oz mixed spice	

Mix all the ingredients to form a fairly stiff dough. Divide into small balls and flatten slightly. Put on a greased baking sheet and bake in a cool oven for about 30 minutes.

* * *

Gingerbread is another Northern delicacy, but for this, oatmeal is not used. There are many varieties of this ancient sweetmeat, which was sold at fairs in medieval times. The cakes were made in fancy shapes and covered in gilt, hence our expression, 'the gilt on the gingerbread'. Now, we usually eat it sliced and buttered.

OLD-FASHIONED YORKSHIRE GINGERBREAD

10oz flour
1 teaspoon ground ginger
½ teaspoon ground cinnamon
1 teaspoon salt
5oz treacle

3oz butter
1 egg
4oz dark brown sugar
¾ teaspoon bicarbonate of soda,
*   dissolved in 3 teaspoons milk*

Mix the flour, ginger, cinnamon and salt. Melt the treacle and butter over a gentle heat, then leave to cool. Beat the egg and sugar together. Add the melted treacle mix alternately with the beaten egg mix to the flour. Add the dissolved bicarbonate of soda and beat to a soft dropping consistency, adding a little more milk if necessary. Bake in a greased 10in-square tin in a slow oven, for 1½ to 2 hours.

STARTFORTH GINGERBREAD

4oz butter
2oz brown sugar
8oz black treacle
8oz plain flour
½ teaspoon bicarbonate of soda

1 teaspoon mixed spice
pinch of ground ginger
2 eggs, beaten
2fl oz sour milk

Melt the butter, sugar and treacle gently. Remove from the heat and stir in the flour sifted with the bicarbonate of soda, spice and ginger. Add the beaten eggs and sour milk, and mix well. Pour into a lined and greased 1lb loaf tin and bake at 350°F (Mark 4) for 1½ to 2 hours.

WAKEFIELD GINGERBREAD

5oz butter
11oz self-raising flour
5oz caster sugar
1½oz chopped mixed peel

2 teaspoons ground ginger
4oz golden syrup
1 dessertspoon brandy

Rub the butter into the flour, add the sugar, peel and ginger. Dissolve the golden syrup in the brandy and mix into the flour mixture; it should have a soft consistency. Put into a greased 8in-square shallow tin and bake in a moderate oven for 1½ hours.

SLEDMERE GINGERBREAD

8oz butter
8oz sugar
8oz treacle
4 eggs

½oz ground ginger
1 teaspoon bicarbonate of soda
1lb flour

Melt the butter, sugar and treacle over a low heat. Beat the eggs and stir in the melted ingredients. Add the ginger and bicarbonate of soda, then mix all into the flour. Bake in a cool oven for 45 minutes.

TREACLE BREAD

2 cups white flour
2 cups brown flour
½ cup brown sugar
1 level teaspoon bicarbonate of soda

2 level teaspoons baking powder
2 eggs
1½ cups dark treacle
1 cup milk
1 cup raisins

Mix the dry ingredients together. Beat the eggs well. Add the eggs, treacle, milk and raisins to the dry mixture, and mix thoroughly. Put into 2 well greased 2lb loaf tins, and bake in a moderate oven for 1 hour. Eat within a week, sliced and buttered.

BLACK TREACLE CAKE

4oz butter
3 cups plain flour
1 cup brown sugar
1 teaspoon salt

1½ teaspoons baking powder
1½ teaspoons bicarbonate of soda
1 cup hot black treacle
2 cups boiling water

Rub the butter into the flour, then add the sugar, salt, baking powder and bicarbonate of soda. Add the hot treacle, then the boiling water. The mixture should have a thick, runny consistency. Bake very slowly (200°F, under Mark ¼) in a lined and greased tin for about 1 hour, until springy to the touch.

* * *

SPICE BUNS

8oz flour
1 teaspoon mixed spice
1 level teaspoon bicarbonate of soda
4oz butter

4oz sugar
2oz candied peel, finely chopped
1 egg, beaten
milk to mix

Sieve the flour with the spice and bicarbonate of soda, rub in the butter. Add the sugar and the peel. Mix the beaten egg with 4 tablespoons milk. Add this to the dry ingredients and mix well. If the mixture is too stiff, add more milk until a soft dropping consistency is obtained. Place spoonfuls in greased bun tins, and bake in a hot oven for about 15 minutes.

GINGER SNAPS

4oz butter
1lb flour
½lb syrup

4oz brown sugar
1 tablespoon ground ginger
1 tablespoon caraway seeds

Rub the butter into the flour, then mix in the syrup, sugar, ginger, and caraway seeds. Work together into a soft dough, and form into small cakes, about 1½in across. Bake on a greased tray in a moderate oven until brown and crisp.

* * *

Brandy Snaps were always sold at the fairs or 'feasts' as they were known in the West Riding. This was the week when all the mills closed down for the annual holiday, and the gypsy people arrived with their travelling fair.

In my town, there was a long approach road to the fairground, and all along it would be stalls selling every kind of sweetmeat and treat. There would be small potatoes, deep-fried on the spot, shovelled into a small bag for a penny, and eaten with the fingers, almost too hot to hold, let alone bite into! There would be the coconut stalls, and the candy floss, huge pink-sugar spun lollipops on sticks; the traditional sweets, big black-and-white-striped humbugs, glittering mounds of coloured boiled sweets, toffee of every kind; and, always, the brandy-snap stalls. Here we bought the rolled-up sticky treacle biscuit which is associated with Wyke, the small town on the Humber that was renamed Kingston upon Hull by Edward the First.

The making of Brandy Snaps calls for a little dexterity!

BRANDY SNAPS

2oz butter
2oz sugar
2 tablespoons golden syrup
2oz flour

1 level teaspoon ground ginger
1 teaspoon brandy
¼ teaspoon grated lemon rind

Melt the fat, sugar and syrup in a pan. Remove from the heat and add the other ingredients. Mix well. Drop teaspoonfuls of the mixture on to a greased baking sheet, about 3in apart. Bake for 7 to 10 minutes in a moderate oven. Remove the sheet from the oven and stand if tor a moment on the top of the stove until a biscuit will lift up when a knife is inserted underneath. Roll the biscuits one at a time round the handle of a wooden spoon, leave a moment to set, then slide off.

Nowadays it seems to be the fashion to fill them with whipped cream, but the fairground people knew no such frivolities.

*   *   *

Apart from the treacly things, Yorkshire offers a great range of other teatime goodies. Many of them were of the 'cut-and-come-again' variety, useful for filling up a cake tin once a week, as my mother did. They were no-nonsense cakes, not often embellished with cream or other delights, tending to be either large richly fruited cakes, or quickly baked small buns.

YORKSHIRE FRUIT LOAF

8oz butter
7oz sugar
3 eggs, beaten
2 tablespoons golden syrup,
*   warmed*
8oz sultanas

8oz currants
2oz mixed peel, chopped
1¼lb self-raising flour
¼ pint milk
½ teaspoon bicarbonate of soda

Cream the butter and sugar, add the beaten eggs, then the warmed syrup. Add the fruit, then the flour, alternating with milk in which the bicarbonate of soda has been dissolved. Pour into 2 large, greased loaf tins, and bake in a moderate oven for 1½ hours. This cake improves with keeping.

PUDDING TIN CAKE

piece of butter the size of an egg
piece of lard the size of an egg
12 tablespoons flour
6 tablespoons sugar
1 teaspoon bicarbonate of soda
grated nutmeg to taste

pinch of salt
2 teaspoons baking powder
1 teaspoon cream of tartar
2 eggs
½ pint milk

Rub the fats into the flour, add the sugar and the rest of the dry ingredients. Break the eggs into the milk, mix well, then add to the dry mixture. Turn into a large, well greased Yorkshire-pudding tin and bake in a moderate oven until risen and brown. A good cake for a large family!

YORKSHIRE DALES CAKE

1lb butter
1lb sugar
8 eggs, well beaten
1¼lb flour
1 nutmeg, grated
1 large teaspoon baking powder

12oz mixed peel
2lb currants
8oz glacé cherries
4oz almonds, chopped
1 large wineglass brandy
grated rind and juice 1 lemon

Beat the butter and sugar, add the beaten eggs, and fold in the other ingredients. Put into 2 greased 2lb loaf tins and bake in a moderate oven for about 4 hours.

PLUM BREAD

4oz lard
4oz butter
2lb flour
4 teaspoons baking powder
1lb soft brown sugar

1lb currants
8oz raisins
4oz candied peel
1 pint milk

Rub the fats into the flour and baking powder, add the sugar and fruits, then mix with the milk to a firm dough. Put into 2 greased 2lb loaf tins and bake in a moderate oven for 1½ to 2 hours.

* * *

Not as bad as it sounds, but a marvellous substitute for a pudding inside a rucksack or lunch box!

HARD CAKE

8oz beef dripping
8oz sugar
4oz currants

1 egg, beaten
little candied peel
flour

Melt the dripping, then add the sugar, currants, egg and peel. Add enough flour to make a firm mix. Pat into a round on a greased baking sheet. Criss-cross with a fork and bake for 1 hour in a moderate oven.

Apart from the famous moor, and the equally famous song about it, there is also this cake—a good, solid concoction, perfect with hot sweet tea at the end of a long walk across the heathered moors!

ILKLEY CAKE

1lb plain flour
¾oz baking powder
½ teaspoon salt
1 teaspoon mixed spice
1 teaspoon ground nutmeg
4oz dripping

4oz raisins
8oz currants
2oz candied peel
12oz brown sugar
milk to mix

Sift together the flour, baking powder, salt and spices. Rub in the dripping. Add the fruit and sugar and mix with milk to a dropping consistency. Turn into a greased 9in cake tin. Bake in a moderately hot oven for 2 hours.

OLD WIFE'S CAKE

8oz butter
8oz sugar
8oz currants
1lb flour

1 teaspoon bicarbonate of soda
½ nutmeg, grated
lemon juice
1 tablespoon milk

Cream the butter and sugar, then add the currants, flour and bicarbonate of soda. Mix in the nutmeg and lemon juice, lastly add the milk. Mix well. Put into 3 well greased 6in tins and bake in a moderate oven for 30 minutes.

BEADLE PLUM CAKE

1lb butter
1lb caster sugar
9 eggs
18oz plain flour
1½ teaspoons baking powder
2 teaspoons mixed spice

8oz raisins
8oz sultanas
8oz currants
4oz mixed peel, finely chopped
grated rind and juice of 1 lemon
a little milk

Cream the butter and sugar until fluffy. Beat the eggs in a bowl over hot water, then whisk into the creamed mix. Sift the flour, baking powder and spice, fold into the mixture. Add the fruit, peel, lemon rind and juice, and mix to a soft dropping consistency, adding a little milk if necessary. Turn into a lined and greased 10in tin, bake for 2 hours at 350°F (Mark 4).

*　*　*

The greatest fruit cake of all, of course, is the Christmas one. In most of Yorkshire, it was a huge affair, laden with fruit and spices, sometimes decorated with a marzipan topping, but hardly ever iced. It was always eaten with an accompaniment of good ripe Wensleydale cheese, a cheese that is, alas, now no longer made in the farmhouses of the Dales. There is one man, however, who was a great cheese-maker until the restrictions of the last war overtook him. Now a country bookseller, his name still evokes a smile and chuckle of pride from the Dales people, and long after the regulations said no, Kit Calvert was making his cheeses, just to give to friends. Indeed, he would say, how can you eat apple pie or Christmas cake without it?

YORKSHIRE CHRISTMAS CAKE

6lb flour	*4lb currants*
1 tablespoon salt	*1½lb raisins*
12oz butter	*1½lb sugar*
12oz lard	*4oz candied peel*
4½oz fresh yeast	*4oz candied orange*
1 pint fresh milk	*grated rind of 1 large lemon*
2 eggs	*grated nutmeg*

Sift the flour and salt, then rub the fats in. Cream the yeast. Add sufficient hot water to the milk to warm it. Beat the eggs and add to the milk and water. Add the yeast to the flour, then add enough liquid to make a light dough. Beat for 20 minutes! Leave to rise for 1½ hours, covered, in a warm place. When well risen, beat in the fruit, sugar, candied fruit, lemon rind and a sprinkling of nutmeg. Knead very thoroughly. Put into 6 greased 1lb loaf tins and bake in a moderate oven until risen and browned.

This recipe is a very old traditional one, but nowadays most people prefer to use the ordinary creamed type of cake recipe.

* * *

Another great favourite at Christmas, especially in the North Riding, was Sour Milk Cake.

SOUR MILK CAKE

8oz butter	*8oz currants*
1lb flour	*2oz mixed peel*
8oz sugar	*1 tablespoon syrup*
1 teaspoon mixed spice	*1 pint sour milk*
1 teaspoon bicarbonate of soda	

Rub the butter into the flour, add all the ingredients except the syrup and milk. Warm the syrup and pour into the centre of the mixture. Mix to a soft dough with the milk. Bake in 2 bread tins in a moderate oven for 1 hour.

YORKSHIRE CAKE

3 teaspoons yeast   *1 pint milk*
2 eggs, beaten   *2lb flour*
4oz butter   *½ teaspoon salt*

Cream the yeast, add the beaten eggs. Melt the butter in the milk, add to the yeast mixture and mix in the flour and salt. Beat well, then leave to rise. Knead and make into 2 cakes. Let them prove then bake on a greased baking sheet in a slow oven.

* * *

And finally, a fruit cake called Yorkshire Soda Cake.

YORKSHIRE SODA CAKE

4oz butter   *1 egg, beaten*
1lb flour   *8oz currants*
½ pint milk   *1 teaspoon bicarbonate of soda*
8oz sugar

Rub the butter into the flour. Mix the milk, sugar and beaten egg together. Add the currants to the flour. Dissolve the bicarbonate of soda in the milk, then add the milk mixture to the flour, stirring to mix. Put in a greased tin and bake at 350°F (Mark 4).

* * *

Seed cakes were a great favourite, and for me, there was one in particular.

MY GRANDMA'S SEEDCAKE

1lb butter   *1 teaspoon cinnamon*
1lb caster sugar   *1 teaspoon ground cloves*
9 eggs   *2oz caraway seeds*
1lb plain flour

Cream the butter and sugar until very fluffy. Beat the eggs in a bowl over hot water, then whisk into the creamed mixture. Sift the flour with the spices, fold into the creamed mix, then add the caraway seeds. Put into a greased, lined, 9in cake tin and bake at 350°F (Mark 4) for 2 hours.

* * *

Another seed cake recipe called for yeast to be used; it was a 'workaday', filling sort of cake, hence its name!

COMMON SEED CAKE

1 tablespoon fresh yeast	*8oz sugar*
2½lb flour	*8oz butter*
½ pint warm milk	*1oz caraway seeds*

Line a square baking tin with greased greaseproof paper. Cream the yeast with a little of the milk and put the mixture into a well in the flour. When bubbling, add the rest of the ingredients, mixing well. Put the mixture into the tin and let it rise. Bake in a hot oven for 1 hour, then brush the top with milk.

* * *

My brother disliked very heavily fruited cakes, even at Christmas, and so my mother would bake a special one for him. It became known as Eddie's Cake.

EDDIE'S CAKE

2oz butter	*8oz flour*
6oz sugar	*6oz currants*
3 eggs, beaten	*2oz candied lemon*
2 teaspoons baking powder	

Cream the butter and sugar, add the beaten eggs. Then add the rest of the ingredients. Bake for 1 hour at 350°F (Mark 4) until nicely golden.

* * *

A cake that boasts of at least three names (and there may be more!) is now a great favourite with my own sons. Mother used to make it, and I always use the name she used for it, that of the small industrial town near the village in which she grew up.

BATLEY CAKE
(also known as COURTING CAKE and RAILWAY SLICE)

12oz plain flour	*1 egg, beaten*
¾oz baking powder	*milk to mix*
½ tablespoon salt	*2oz jam, warmed*
6oz butter	*beaten egg*
6oz caster sugar	*sugar*

Sift the flour, baking powder and salt together, rub in the butter, then add the sugar. Mix to a stiff dropping consistency with the egg and a little milk. Divide the mixture into 2. Roll into rounds ½in thick. Spread the warmed jam on one half, cover with the other. Pinch the edges together, brush with beaten egg and sprinkle liberally with sugar. Bake in a swiss roll tin at 350°F (Mark 4) for 30 minutes.

❄   ❄   ❄

Grandma had another speciality, one which mother never made, either because it took too much time, or it was too great a luxury.

GRANDMA'S SPONGE CAKE

3 eggs	*1 teaspoon baking powder*
4oz caster sugar	*caster sugar*
4oz flour	

Grease a sponge cake mould with butter, dredge with caster sugar, and shake out the surplus. Whisk the eggs well, add the sugar, and whisk again until thick and creamy. Mix the flour and baking powder, and fold into the creamed mix very lightly. Turn into the mould, filling it about two-thirds full. Bake in a gentle oven until firm to the touch. As soon as the cake wrinkles on top and shrinks from the sides of the tin, it is ready.

This one was probably a comfort to those who had just 'taken the waters' in this beautiful spa town of Yorkshire. It no doubt helped to take away the taste of the mineral-rich water, but could hardly have helped with the fat problem.

HARROGATE SPONGE CAKE

4 eggs
4oz caster sugar
2 tablespoons boiling water

4oz plain flour, sifted
¾ teaspoon baking powder

Beat the eggs and sugar in a bowl over hot water. When thick and creamy, add the boiling water and whisk for a further 5 minutes. Fold in half the sifted flour and baking powder, then add the rest. Grease 2 8in sandwich tins and dust with sugar. Spoon in the mixture. Bake for 20 minutes at 375°F (Mark 5). When cold, sandwich with jam or cream and dust the top with icing sugar.

YORKSHIRE SANDWICH CAKE

2oz plain flour
2oz ground rice
pinch of salt
1 teaspoon baking powder

2oz butter
2oz caster sugar
1 egg, beaten
milk to mix

Sieve the flour, ground rice and salt together. Take 1 tablespoon of this and add the baking powder, keeping it separate from the rest of the flour mix. Cream the butter and sugar until fluffy, add the beaten egg, then beat well. Add the bulk of the flour mix, with enough milk to make a dropping consistency. Beat again, then add the tablespoon of flour and baking powder. Pour into greased sandwich tins, and bake in a hot oven for 15 minutes. When cold, sandwich together with jam.

PLAIN JAM SANDWICH

3oz butter
3oz sugar
6oz flour

3 eggs, beaten
1 teaspoon baking powder
jam and sugar

Cream the butter and sugar, add the flour and beaten eggs alternately. Beat until smooth, adding the baking powder last. Put into a greased and lined sandwich tin and bake in a hot oven for 7 to 10 minutes. Turn out to cool. When cold, split into 2 layers, lay them on sugared paper and spread with jam. Put the halves together again and dust with sugar.

※　※　※

Along with the bigger cakes, there were always buns, the name given to any small cake in Yorkshire, whether it was made with treacle or sugar, was fruited or not. The highly decorative small cakes sold in shops were referred to as 'fancies'. These were treats not experienced too often, and we contented ourselves with the buns of baking day. One of my own favourites was Sly Cakes.

SLY CAKES

1lb flour	*8oz butter*
2oz sugar	*8oz currants (or jam)*
water	*6 drops lemon essence*

Mix the flour and sugar then make into a smooth paste (not too wet) with a little water and the lemon essence. Roll out and spread with dabs of butter as if for puff pastry, rolling three times. Finally, roll very thinly and cut into rounds. Spread half the rounds with currants or jam, very thickly. Press the other rounds on top and bake on a greased baking sheet in a hot oven until golden.

These are very short and crumbly, as are the following.

※　※　※

This is Richmond in Yorkshire of course, and nothing to do with the 'Maids of Honour' Richmond.

RICHMOND SHORT CAKES

12oz butter	*8oz currants*
2lb flour	*1 nutmeg, grated*
8oz sugar	*lemon juice*

94

Melt the butter, then pour into the mixed dry ingredients. Mix to a stiff paste, adding a little lemon juice. Roll out into a large, flattish round, and score the top with a diamond pattern. Sprinkle with sugar and bake on a greased baking sheet in a moderate oven for about 30 minutes, until golden brown.

As Yorkshire is such a big county, we do not have the usual Queen Cakes; ours are called King Cakes.

KING CAKES

12oz butter	*8oz currants*
1lb flour	*8oz sugar*
egg yolk	*ground mace, to taste*

Rub the butter into the flour. Add enough egg yolk to make the mixture soft, then add the other ingredients. Put into cake papers and bake at 300°F (Mark 2) for 7 to 10 minutes.

RICE CAKES

2 eggs	*4oz ground rice*
4oz sugar	

Beat the eggs well, add the sugar and beat well again. Add the ground rice, beat again. Put into buttered bun tins and bake at 350°F (Mark 4) for about 30 minutes.

COBURG BUNS

6oz flour	*4oz butter*
1 teaspoon ground ginger	*3oz caster sugar*
½ teaspoon ground nutmeg	*2 eggs*
½ teaspoon cinnamon	*2 teaspoons syrup*
½ teaspoon bicarbonate of soda	*flaked almonds*

Sieve the flour, spices and bicarbonate of soda together. Cream the butter and sugar, add the beaten eggs and mix into the dry ingredients (do not beat). Add the syrup. Put some flaked almonds in the bottoms of buttered bun tins and cover with the mixture. Bake in a hot oven until nicely golden.

CABLE CAKES

2oz caster sugar
4oz lard
1lb plain flour
1oz baking powder

1lb mincemeat
2 eggs
5fl oz milk

Cream the sugar and lard until light, add the sifted flour and baking powder, then the mincemeat. Beat the eggs with the milk and stir into the mixture to make a stiffish dough. Spoon into greased bun tins and bake in a hot oven at 450°F (Mark 8) for 15 minutes.

* * *

Wennington is a small village in Lancashire (dare it be said?!), but it lies so near to the Craven district of the old West Riding, adjacent to the Lancashire border, that, like hotpot, its origins are lost. And some good things do come out of Lancashire, even a Yorkshire tyke will admit that!

WENNINGTON CAKES

6oz butter
8oz flour
3 eggs, beaten

a few currants, or chopped
almonds
8oz lump sugar
grated rind of 1 lemon

Rub the butter into the flour, then add the beaten egg. Add the other ingredients and mix to a soft dropping consistency. Place in heaps on a greased baking sheet and bake at 350°F (Mark 4) for about 10 minutes.

* * *

Biscuits were not baked very often in my part of the world, being too time-consuming and fiddly. In any case, we had one or two very good commercial biscuit-makers in the West Riding. But for special occasions there were a few old recipes, apart from the brandy snaps of feast days. A very old one was for biscuits to be served at funerals. These were handed round to the mourners and friends before the actual service, and should any be left over they were put into twists of paper for the children to take home. They were baked in rounds, then cut in halves, and always offered in white paper.

FUNERAL BISCUITS

3 eggs   *8oz flour*
8oz sugar

Beat the eggs and sugar for 20 minutes (this before the days of mixers!). Add the flour, mix well, then leave to stand for 1 hour. Drop in tablespoonfuls on to pieces of greased greaseproof paper on a baking sheet. Cook in a fairly hot oven until firm but not brown. The tops will be sugary.

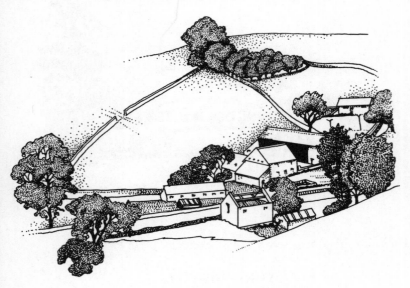

For teatime when the parson came to tea, as he did each Sunday in turn to his parishioners, something delicate was called for, and although the poor man would no doubt have appreciated a large piece of fruit cake, he was often given small delicacies called Rout Cakes.

ROUT CAKES

1lb flour	*3 eggs*
8oz currants	*1 teaspoon rose-water*
8oz butter	*1 teaspoon orange-water*
8oz caster sugar	*1 tablespoon Madeira*

Sift the flour and mix in the currants. Cream the butter and sugar until fluffy. Beat in the eggs one at a time. Add the flour alternately with the rose- and orange-waters, and the Madeira. Dust a baking sheet with flour and sugar, drop the stiffish mixture on, in little heaps. Bake in a hot oven. The cakes cook in a few minutes, and are about the size of a fifty-pence piece.

He might also be offered York Biscuits.

YORK BISCUITS

6oz butter	*1½ teaspoons baking powder*
6oz caster sugar	*5fl oz milk*
1lb plain flour	

Beat the butter and sugar until fluffy, fold in the sifted flour and baking powder, then mix to a stiff dough with milk. Knead well. Roll out thinly, cut into 2 rounds, and bake on a greased baking sheet for 30 minutes at 325°F (Mark 3).

And finally, a biscuit to be eaten with hot cocoa.

CRACKNELLS

2oz butter
8oz sugar
8oz flour

2 eggs
1oz caraway seeds

Cream the butter and sugar, add the flour. Beat in the eggs, add the caraway seeds and work into a paste. Roll out as thinly as possible and cut into rounds with a fluted cutter. Lay on a greased baking sheet and bake in a slow oven.

Eat on a bitterly cold night, with a good Yorkshire east wind whistling around the chimney pots, and dip them into hot cocoa!

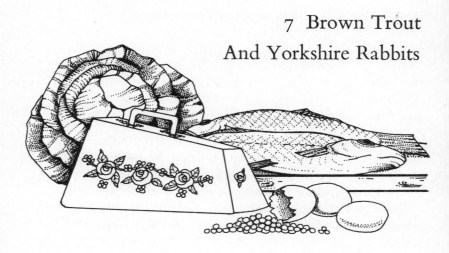

There are not many old recipes for fish dishes special to York-shire, possibly due to the cost of transport from the sea inland, but there are some traditional ones that use the fish caught in the swift mountain becks. Crayfish were abundant but, sadly, seem to have died out in recent years. These were never the monster crayfish sold for their tails, but small delicate ones that lurked in the peaty brown waters running off the moors. If you know where to look it is still possible to find some, but canny Yorkshire folk never tell secrets like that.

Usually found in August, the crayfish were traditionally cooked over an open fire and eaten with lemon juice and butter. After being boiled rapidly in salted water for about twelve minutes, they were rinsed in cold water then removed from their shells. Delicious eaten cold with lemon and brown bread, or put under the grill to heat through, and served with melted butter and lemon juice. As the 'season' for them was so short, potting them meant that they could be enjoyed a little longer.

POTTED CRAYFISH

Pick out the meat from the boiled crayfish, pound (or liquidise) into a paste, seasoning with mace, pepper and salt. Put into pots, cover with clarified butter, and another cover, firmly tied.

Trout of course also run in the same hill streams, and were a treat for tea at many farms, served simply fried in coarse oatmeal and butter.

Fish from the sea were mainly haddock, herrings or hake which was always popular in the West Riding, especially with my mother! She would simply fry her piece of fish in hardly any butter, then eat it with lemon juice or vinegar. Another good way to cook hake is with onions.

HAKE STEAKS AND ONIONS

Fry sliced onions in good dripping until soft. Put steaks of fish, each about 6oz in weight, on top of the onions and season with salt and pepper. Put a small piece of butter on each fish steak. Add a little water, cover and cook in a moderate oven for 30 minutes. Serve with mashed potatoes.

* * *

Plain grilled hake served with gooseberry sauce was another favourite, and ling, a member of the cod family, was the base for a good filling dish.

LING PIE

1lb ling	*salt and pepper*
1oz seasoned flour	*½ pint milk*
4oz bacon, chopped	*12oz puff pastry*
2 hard-boiled eggs, sliced	*beaten egg*
2oz chopped onions	

Cut the fish into serving portions, coat with seasoned flour. Place in a buttered 2½ pint pie dish. Layer with bacon, eggs and onions, then season. Pour the milk over, cover with a pastry lid and brush with beaten egg. Bake for 10 minutes at 425°F (Mark 7) then for 15 minutes at 350°F (Mark 4).

* * *

From the east coast of Yorkshire came the haddock, the fish that is the mainstay of the fish and chip shops that spread down from Scotland to cover the whole of England. They remain firm favourites of the Yorkshire people, despite the various 'take-away' booms, and even quite small Dales villages still boast their own chip shop.

Most of the old recipes never included batter, which may have helped to increase the demand for the shop-fried variety.

HUMBER HADDOCK

2lb haddock fillets	¾ pint milk
¾lb tomatoes	1oz butter
salt and pepper	8oz mushrooms, sliced

Skin and de-seed the tomatoes. Wipe the fish and place in a buttered dish. Cover with seasoning and milk. Dice the tomato pulp and add to the fish, with the mushrooms. Dot with butter. Cover with buttered paper and bake at 350°F (Mark 4) for about 15 minutes.

This can also be made with smoked haddock, which is used for the following recipe.

FINNAN HADDOCK PASTY

2oz flour	1 tablespoon white sauce
1oz margarine	parsley
1oz cheese, grated	beaten egg
salt and pepper	1 tablespoon grated cheese
4oz finnan haddock, cooked and shredded	

Make a pastry with the flour, margarine, cheese and seasoning. Roll out into 2 rounds. Mix the rest of the ingredients into a filling, putting half on to each pastry round. Wet the edges of the rounds and fold over like a Cornish pasty. Bake in a hot oven for 15 minutes.

* * *

Plaice makes the basis for another West Riding dish.

CHEESY PLAICE

4 fillets plaice	*2oz cheese, grated*
4oz mushrooms	*salt and pepper*
1oz flour	*4 tomatoes*
1oz margarine	*sugar*
½ pint milk	*breadcrumbs*

Skin the fillets of fish, roll up and put on a greased plate. Steam for 20 minutes over boiling water. Put into a greased baking dish. Fry the mushrooms and place at each end of the fish. Make a cheese sauce with the flour, margarine, milk, cheese and seasoning, then pour over the fish and mushrooms. Slice and fry the tomatoes, lay them at the ends of the dish and sprinkle with a little sugar. Sprinkle breadcrumbs all over and brown under a hot grill.

* * *

Salmon was for high days and treats, and the tinned variety invariably made its appearance for Sunday tea. Just occasionally, fresh salmon might be not too expensive in the market, and then we could eat it baked.

BAKED SALMON WITH CUCUMBER

slices of fresh salmon	*1 tablespoon white wine*
2oz butter per 1lb fish	*1 cucumber*
juice of 1 lemon	*finely chopped parsley*

Lay the salmon slices in a well buttered pie dish. Add the butter, lemon juice and white wine. (My mother would not put this ingredient into it, but a very little white vinegar was a rough substitute or, better still, cider.) Cover the dish with buttered paper and bake in a moderate oven for 20 minutes. Peel and cube the cucumber. Cook until tender, drain off the liquid. Put the cucumber into a serving dish, sqeeze lemon juice over, then sprinkle with finely chopped parsley. Place the salmon slices around the cucumber. Strain the juices from the fish all over and serve hot.

SALMON MOULD

1 medium tin salmon
4 tablespoons vinegar
½oz gelatine, dissolved in 3
  tablespoons hot water

pinch of ground mace
salt and pepper

Mix all the ingredients together and when nearly setting, pour into a wetted mould. Turn out when firm. Serve with tiny new potatoes.

* * *

Herrings were good and cheap, either fresh or cured.

SOLOMON GUNDY FOR LENT

6 fresh herrings
4oz anchovies
1 large apple, peeled and grated

a little grated onion
lemon peel

Soak the herrings in water overnight. Boil in fresh water until soft. Carefully remove the flesh, leaving the head, tail and bones intact. Mix the fish meat with the anchovies, apple, onion and lemon peel. Mix well, then lay over the fish bone, making a fish shape. Lay long thin strips of lemon peel across the fish. Serve cold with brown bread and butter.

HOME-MADE BLOATER PASTE (superb on toast)

6 large bloaters
10oz butter

3 dessertspoons anchovy sauce
cayenne and white pepper

Put the bloaters into boiling water for 10 minutes. Then cut off the heads, skin them and take out the bones. Pound the flesh to a pulp with the butter, sauce and peppers to taste. Put into small pots and seal with clarified butter.

YORKSHIRE KIPPER PASTE

2 large kippers
10oz unsalted butter

2 hard-boiled eggs

Stand the kippers head down in a jug of hot water. Leave for 10 minutes. Drain, remove the skin and bones. Pound with the butter and eggs. Put into small pots, cool, then seal with clarified butter.

*　*　*

Cheese played an important part in the Yorkshire diet, naturally, since every Dales farm made its own fine cheeses. Apart from being eaten with pies and cake, it was also used in cooking. The most famous cooked cheese recipe has to be Yorkshire Rabbit—a variation on Welsh Rabbit—in which, oddly enough, the most favoured cheese is Lancashire! Lancashire has a good cooking texture, melting rather than going into strings. In any case, as one old Dales farmer once said to me, 'Tha mun nivver spoil a good bit o' Wensleydale wi' cookin' it!'

YORKSHIRE RABBIT

1lb Lancashire cheese, grated　　*salt and pepper*
5fl oz milk　　*8 slices toast*
2oz butter　　*8 poached eggs*
½ teaspoon made mustard

Put the cheese into a shallow pan with the milk, butter, mustard and seasoning. Stir over a very low heat until it is the consistency of thick cream. Pour over the toast, brown under a grill and top with poached eggs.

*　*　*

A variation on this is simply called Cheese Paste, and may be very much older in origin.

CHEESE PASTE

1 tablespoon butter　　*1 egg yolk, beaten*
4oz cheese, grated　　*cup of cream*
pinch of cayenne pepper　　*Yorkshire Relish*

Melt the butter in a pan. Add the cheese and cayenne pepper. Stir until the cheese has melted, then gradually stir in the beaten egg yolk, thinned with the cream. Add Yorkshire Relish to taste. Stir until thick and smooth, then pot up. Use as a savoury spread on toast.

❋   ❋   ❋

In the farmhouses, where milk was plentiful, the surplus would be made into cream cheese. An old traditional recipe needs time and care but produces a delicious end result.

YORKSHIRE CREAM CHEESE

Stand 1 pint thin cream in a basin for 12 hours. Stir in a good pinch of salt. Put into an old clean dinner napkin and hang up in a cool place for 24 hours. (Keep a bowl underneath for drips.) Take down, turn inside out, tie and hang for another 24 hours. It is now ready to press. If you have no dairy press, get a small wooden box with holes bored in the bottom. Get a strip of huckaback towelling, enough to lay across the sides and bottom, and fold over. Scald it in boiling water, then run cold water over it. Lay it in the box, and over it, a piece of butter muslin. Press in the cream, fold muslin over, then the huckaback. Put on the lid, which must fit inside the box. Stand the box so that the whey can run clear at the bottom, put a heavy weight on to the lid and leave for 24 hours.

❋   ❋   ❋

There was also the curd, needed for curd tarts.

CURD CHEESE

Put 1 quart milk into a basin with the strained juice of 3 lemons. Let mixture stand for 12 hours in a warm room. Put a large square of muslin over another basin, pour the curds into this. Tie round with string, and hang to drain. When it has stopped dripping, put the solids between 2 plates, weight the top one, and leave to press out any remaining moisture. Turn out and shape into a mould.

This is absolutely delicious eaten with strawberries! But its best use is for cheesecake.

TRADITIONAL YORKSHIRE CHEESECAKE

½ *pint curds*	*1 spoon ratafia*
4 eggs	*4oz currants*
3 spoons thick cream	*8oz puff pastry*
¼ *nutmeg, grated*	

Beat the curds with the eggs, cream, grated nutmeg, ratafia and currants. Put into small pans lined with puff pastry. Bake at 350°F (Mark 4) until set.

❋ ❋ ❋

Eggs were never my favourite food as a child, probably because I was faced with one beaten up in milk each day on my return from school! As a very young child, I was considered 'delicate', suffering nearly every common childhood disease, as well as scarlet fever and diphtheria with their enforced stays in isolation hospitals. After a terrific argument with the local Health Officer my mother took me out of the last hospital, with cross eyes and legs that would not hold me up. She pushed me around in a borrowed wheelchair for six months, and proceeded to 'build me up'.

The beaten egg was always sticky and not beaten sufficiently, so that I swallowed horrible lumps of gooey white, and each day I dreaded four o'clock. The result was that I began to hate all eggs, and it was not until my teens, when I took to fell walking, that I could appreciate a boiled egg for tea. But mother must have been right, since I am still fell walking!

Grandma, however, had a nice way with eggs, one that had no name but which she called her Pretty Dish.

PRETTY DISH

Break some eggs into a small pie dish without breaking the yolks. Drop warm melted butter over them and sprinkle with breadcrumbs. Put into the oven until the whites are set, and surround with a ring of chopped parsley before eating.

And another she called Browned Eggs.

BROWNED EGGS

8 hard-boiled eggs, shelled   *fried bread*
thick brown gravy   *parsley*

Lay 3 of the eggs in a dish with the gravy. Cut the rest into halves, and set them facing upwards around the others. Arrange triangles of fried bread around the eggs and garnish with parsley. Serve very hot.

*   *   *

When there was a glut of eggs, they were put down to pickle.

PICKLED EGGS

16 hard-boiled eggs   *½oz allspice*
1 quart vinegar   *½oz root ginger*
½oz black peppercorns

Remove the egg shells. Put the eggs into a wide-necked jar. Boil the peppercorns, allspice and root ginger in the vinegar for 10 minutes. Whilst still boiling, strain over the eggs. When cold, cover closely and store in a cool, dry place. They are ready in 2 weeks.

*   *   *

Again using a surplus of eggs, a kind of baked custard that is a little different, as is its name.

YORKSHIRE WIFE'S SOD

5 large eggs   *2 oatcakes*
1½ pints milk   *butter*

Beat the eggs for 2 minutes. Add the milk, and season. Mix well. Grease a baking pan with butter and pour in the mix. Break up the oatcakes into ½in pieces, then sprinkle on top of the 'sod'. Add small pieces of butter and bake for 20 minutes in a moderate oven. This is even nicer if the oatcakes are first toasted and buttered.

Yorkshire vegetables are like the Scottish ones, sturdy and filling. Only in later times have the exotic peppers, courgettes and aubergines appeared on the market stalls. Until now, Yorkshire folk were content with their turnips and cabbage, and of course the famous mushy peas.

Mushy peas were always sold at the fish and chip shops and, quite often, in special 'pie and peas' shops, where a small pork pie, surrounded by a sea of dull green, mushy peas, was a treat know to us as a 'swimmer'. There was not often enough money for us all to buy one of these, but one of the 'gang', the children living in the same street, would sometimes go down to the old cafe known as the Criterion, and buy a swimmer to share. Now of course, mushy peas come in cans.

MUSHY PEAS THE OLD WAY

Soak some dried peas overnight, with 1 dessertspoon bicarbonate of soda added to the water. Next day, strain, put them into fresh water with a little salt and sugar, and cook very slowly. The old side ovens were perfect for producing beautifully mushy peas; the important thing is the long, very slow cooking. Eat with salt, pepper and a sprinkling of vinegar.

* * *

Turnips—swedes in the South—were a good stand-by in the winter and went well with the Sunday roast beef.

MASHED TURNIPS (Swedes)

Peel, cut into pieces, boil until soft. Mash with plenty of butter and black pepper, leaving no lumps!

* * *

Parsnips were often mashed, after being boiled until tender, with a little 'top of the milk' and pepper. Or they could be cut into long pieces, parboiled, then fried in good dripping like chips. Delicious with roast pork.

The humble potato was always given royal treatment in our

household, there was no mere boiling and serving up in lumps for us! Mother always took great care to make the potatoes a fitting accompaniment to whatever else she was serving.

POTATOES THE YORKSHIRE WAY

Cover the peeled potatoes with cold water, boil slowly until tender but not mushy. Drain, add salt, then leave the uncovered pan on a very low heat, shaking furiously every minute or so, until ready to serve. In this way, the potatoes remain dry and floury.

If required mashed, add lots of butter, 'top of the milk' and an egg to the boiled potatoes, then mash thoroughly.

*   *   *

Cabbage was steamed rather than boiled, and when cooked, chopped up with a good knob of butter and plenty of pepper. Leeks were plainly boiled, served with butter, or baked in butter or stock in the oven. In winter, near Christmas time, when the celery men appeared in the market, there would be fried celery.

FRIED CELERY

3 heads of celery	*ground nutmeg*
2 eggs, separated	*2oz flour*
4 teaspoons lemon juice	*2oz lard*
½ teaspoon salt	*2oz butter*

Cut the green tops from the celery, remove the outer stalks and wash the rest well in running water. Beat the egg yolks, lemon juice, salt and nutmeg, mix in the flour and gently fold in the whipped egg whites. Dip each head of celery into this batter, and fry in the hot lard. Serve very hot, with melted butter poured over.

*   *   *

Lastly, another winter vegetable that can stand the harsh Yorkshire climate.

KALE

2lb kale
1oz butter
1 tablespoon cream

2 tablespoons stock
salt and pepper

Pick the leaves from the stalks, and cook in boiling salted water until tender. Drain and sieve. Put back into the pan with the butter, cream, stock and seasoning. Shake well and serve.

*　*　*

8 Feast Days
And Squirrel Days

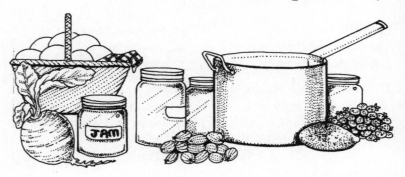

The art of the squirrel is alive and well in Yorkshire, as in most parts of the country; jams and preserves have always been a real part of kitchen life, especially in the rural areas. For mother, deep in the heavy industrial part of the county, there was not much choice, since the colder climate does not encourage widespread orcharding. But being near to Morley and Leeds, she was always sure of one fruit—rhubarb, and this helped along the preserves greatly.

RHUBARB JAM 1

8lb rhubarb
8lb loaf sugar

1lb candied peel
4 level teaspoons ground ginger

Cut the rhubarb into 1in pieces. Put into a pan, crush the sugar slightly and spread over the fruit. Leave until the next day. Cut the peel thinly, then add with the ginger to the fruit and sugar. Boil up until the mixture turns a nice red colour (about 1½ hours). Pour into scalded, dry jars and cover.

RHUBARB JAM 2

8lb rhubarb, peeled
8lb sugar

1lb minced lemon peel

Cut the peeled rhubarb into 1in lengths. Layer the fruit and sugar in a pan. Leave for 5 days, then boil for 30 minutes. Add the minced peel and continue to boil until setting point is reached, about 15 minutes more. Pot up as usual.

This recipe was no doubt useful to the farmer's wife, since she could help with any chores on the farm whilst the fruit and sugar soaked.

PRESERVED RHUBARB

Wash some rhubarb and cut into 2in pieces. Add 1lb sugar to each 1lb of fruit, put into a bowl and stand for 3 days. Boil for 20 minutes, adding a little lemon juice and a small piece of root ginger. Put into pots when thick, and cover.

RHUBARB CHUTNEY

2lb rhubarb, cut into 1in lengths
8oz sugar
3 onions, minced
4oz stoned raisins

2 tablespoons salt
1 tablespoon curry powder
½ teaspoon cayenne pepper
½ pint malt vinegar

Gently stew the fruit with the sugar. When soft, add the rest of the ingredients, and stir over the heat until nice and thick. Put into jars and tie down.

* * *

There were always apples too, to be made into apple pies, *purée* which was bottled for later use as apple sauce, and a delicious something called Apple Ginger.

APPLE GINGER,

4lb sugar
1 quart water
4lb apples, peeled, cored and
* chopped*

2oz preserved ginger

Boil the sugar and water for 25 minutes, until syrupy. Add the apples, still boiling quickly all the time and stirring to prevent sticking. Add the ginger. Boil all together fast, until the mixture clears, skimming occasionally. Put into basins or jars and tie down.

This is quite delicious eaten with fresh cream, or it can be used for a traditional Christmas side dish.

OLD ENGLISH APPLE CAKE

1lb apple ginger   *chopped almonds*
whipped cream

Fill a fancy mould with apple ginger, allow to take the shape, then turn out carefully. Decorate with whipped cream and almonds.

＊　＊　＊

The small hard 'stewing' pears that grow in old gardens were made into a marmalade.

PEAR MARMALADE

6lb small hard pears   *4lb sugar*

Put the pears into a pan with sufficient cold water to cover. Cover the pan and cook gently until the fruit is soft. Cool the pears in cold water. Peel, core and quarter them, put into another pan, add 3 teacups water and place over a gentle heat. Mash the fruit down, add the sugar, stir, then simmer until thick. Pot as usual.

＊　＊　＊

The sturdy crab apple grows all over Yorkshire, and although we scrumped the bitterly tart fruit, we only managed to get stomach-ache. The rest went home to be pickled.

PICKLED CRAB APPLES

2lb crab apples
1 pint vinegar
8oz sugar
6 cloves

pinch of ground cinnamon
1 teaspoon mixed pickling
spice, tied in muslin

Wash the fruit and remove the stalks. Put the vinegar, sugar, cloves, cinnamon and spice in a pan, heat until the sugar dissolves. Add the apples and simmer until slightly softened. Take out the fruit and place in a Kilner jar. Remove the bag of spice, then boil up the liquid until it thickens. Pour over the apples and seal down. When matured, the fruit will have softened completely.

❋   ❋   ❋

Grandma's redcurrant jelly was another treat. She called it a quidny of currants and the recipe was a very old family one, never really written down but 'talked' through the generations.

CURRANT QUIDNY

Put redcurrants into a jar with a spoonful or two of water, cover, then stand the jar in boiling water. When the fruit has softened, strain, and to every pint of juice add 1lb loaf sugar. Boil until it jells, then pot it.

❋   ❋   ❋

The rowan tree is a tree of the North. Not too tall, and always bending in the prevailing wind, its bright-red berries are a lovely sight in late summer. Out on the moors and fells, where other trees do not grow, the rowan finds a crag against which to brace itself, and I have often seen fine specimens growing on the very edges of enormous potholes, their berries temptingly out of reach, unless one risked a rapid descent into the bowels of the limestone cave system! A rowan tree is often planted in a garden to 'keep away the witches', and after its bright show of blossoms in the spring, followed by the brilliant red berries, there is still joy to come, in Rowan Jelly.

ROWAN JELLY

Wash the ripe berries and boil in sufficient water to cover, until soft (about 30 minutes). Put the berries into a jelly bag, crushing them slightly. Leave overnight. Put the juice into a preserving pan, and add sugar, allowing 1lb for each pint of juice. Boil until it jells. Pour into jars and seal. Rowan Jelly improves with keeping, and can be stored for 2 years at least.

*　*　*

Wild raspberries also grow in the old West Riding, but speed was essential if you were to gather them first, as they were not too common!

RASPBERRY PRESERVE

4lb raspberries　　　　　　　*5lb sugar*

Put the fruit on a large dish, the sugar on another. Put both into a hot oven. When very hot, remove and beat the fruit thoroughly. Gradually add the hot sugar, beating all well until the sugar has dissolved. Then put into jars. This preserve keeps for a long time and has all the flavour of the fresh fruit.

Something else that will keep for as long as 3 years, if you can resist it, is a lemon curd.

OLD FASHIONED LEMON CHEESE

1lb loaf sugar　　　　　　　*8 egg yolks*
3 lemons　　　　　　　　　　*5 egg whites*

Put the sugar into a thick saucepan, add the finely grated rind of 2 lemons, and the juice of 3. Put over low heat until the sugar dissolves. Beat the egg yolks and whites separately, then add to the sugar syrup. Stir all together over low heat until the mixture thickens. Pot and cover.

*　*　*

Pickles, chutneys, relishes and such always bring to mind a favourite 'party piece' of mine, usually performed at Christmas when all the family gathered at Grandfather's house. After tea, there would be a call for a 'turn', and each of us would try to entertain the rest. My small effort, long forgotten as far as the exact wording, brings a smile whenever I eat sandwiches made with meat. For during my small act, I would be found crying, and when asked what the trouble was, would sob, 'Me mate— I've lost me mate'. Consternation all round, as grown-ups pretended to search for a missing friend, until in mock desperation, I would bellow, 'No, no! Me mate—me *mate*—out of me sandwich!'

The cold meat left over from the Sunday dinner would be eaten with sauces and pickles. Apart from our famous thick Yorkshire Relish (there was a thin version, to be eaten with chips!), there would be home-made ones.

OLD RELISH

4 shallots	1 tablespoon anchovies
2 tablespoons soy	few cloves
3 cloves garlic	¾oz cayenne pepper
1 large tablespoon brown sugar	1 quart vinegar

Chop the shallots. Pound all the other ingredients, excluding the vinegar, then add the shallots. Put into a glazed stoneware jar with the vinegar and cork lightly.

The jar would be left in a convenient place so that everyone passing it could give it a shake! After a month of this treatment, it was then strained into bottles.

YORKSHIRE SAUCE

rind and juice of 3 oranges	6oz redcurrant jelly
¾ pint port	1½oz brown sauce
½ teaspoon cinnamon	salt and pepper

Cut the orange rind, with no pith, into thin strips. Heat in the port for a few minutes. Strain, add the cinnamon, jelly and sauce. Heat, and add the orange juice and seasoning before serving, very hot, with duck or game.

SAUCE FOR A GOOSE

Scald some gooseberries and mix with sorrel juice and a little butter. Sweeten to taste, then heat but do not boil.

BEETROOT PICKLE

Boil some beetroots until tender. Remove the skin whilst hot, then slice thinly. Put a layer in a dish, sprinkle with sugar and add a little vinegar. Repeat layers, without using too much vinegar, until all the beetroot has been used.

YORKSHIRE PLOUGHBOY

1 tablespoon treacle
2 tablespoons vinegar
¼ teaspoon black pepper
1 red cabbage, finely shredded
1 onion, finely shredded

Mix the treacle, vinegar and pepper together, and stir into the vegetables. Eat with cold meat and jacket potatoes.

* * *

This is not exactly a relish, but without it, where would our roast pork have been?

YORKSHIRE STUFFING

4oz fresh white breadcrumbs
2oz currants
ground mace and sage
salt and pepper

Soak the breadcrumbs in hot water, then squeeze as dry as possible. Mix with the currants and seasonings, and use to stuff a pork joint.

CREAM SALAD

1 lettuce, finely shredded
1 bunch spring onions, chopped
¼ pint thick cream
salt and vinegar to taste
1 teaspoon sugar

Mix all the ingredients together, and serve with cold beef and hot new potatoes.

Finally, the drinks cupboard was never forgotten when preserving time came round. For those long hot summer days of the past, there would be ample supplies of mother's lemon barley water, made in great jugfuls, and a useful stand-by for feverish colds.

LEMON BARLEY WATER

1oz pearl barley   *grated rind and juice of 1 lemon*
1 quart water   *sugar to taste*

Boil the barley and water for 1 hour. Strain out the barley, then add the lemon rind and juice to the water. Sweeten to taste and leave until cold. Before drinking, strain out the rind.

GREEN GOOSEBERRY WINE

hard green gooseberries   *French brandy*
loaf sugar   *isinglass*

Bruise the unripe fruit. To 1lb of fruit, add 1 quart cold water. Let it stand for 3 days, stirring twice daily. Strain, then to 1 gallon of juice, add 3lb loaf sugar. Put into a cask, and to every 20 quarts of liquor add 1 quart French brandy, and a little isinglass. Taste in 6 months, and if the sweetness has gone, bottle the wine and wire down the corks.

GILLIFLOWER SYRUP

5 pints gilliflowers (wallflowers)   loaf sugar
2 pints water

Add 2 pints boiling water to the flowers, place in an earthen-ware pot. Leave for a day and a night. Strain. To 1 quart of liquor, add 1½lb loaf sugar. Boil over a slow heat, skimming away any scum, until syrupy. Bottle when cold.

For Dandelion Wine, only the first dandelions of the season are used, and obviously the more remote the spot you can pick them from, the better!

DANDELION WINE

6 pints dandelion flower heads   demerara sugar
6 oranges   1oz fresh yeast on small piece of
3 lemons   toast
6 quarts boiling water

Squeeze the oranges and lemons, reserve the juice. Boil the pulp and skins, and half the dandelion flowers in the water for 45 minutes. Pour on to the rest of the flowers and leave to stand until cold. Strain. Bring the liquid back to the boil, then add 4lb demerara sugar to every gallon of liquid. Put into an earthenware bowl, add the yeast and toast, yeast downwards. Let it stand for 4 days. Add the fruit juices and put into a cask or barrel. Bottle after 6 months. This is a golden wine, and if you can manage to keep it for 4 or 5 years, it tastes like champagne!

CELERY WINE

4lb celery, green ends and leaves   1oz fresh yeast
1 gallon water   toast
4lb sugar

Wash the celery well, then boil in the water until tender. Strain out the celery. Add the sugar to the liquid. When cool, add the yeast on a small piece of toast, then leave for 3 days. Strain into a stone jar, cork loosely for 3 months. Then bottle for use. This wine improves with keeping and is said to be good for rheumatism.

MOCK PORT

4lb beetroot
4 quarts cold water
loaf sugar

lemon juice
cloves
root ginger

Wash the beetroot carefully, cut into pieces quickly, and put into the water. Boil until all the colour has been extracted, then strain off the liquid. To every quart of liquid, add ½lb loaf sugar, the juice of 1 lemon, 4 cloves and a small piece of bruised root ginger. Stir until the sugar has dissolved, then leave covered for 2 weeks. The wine can then be bottled, but cork lightly until fermentation has ceased. A little brandy added is an improvement, but not necessary. Do not drink for 1 year.

NETTLE BEER (for more mundane occasions!)

season's first young nettle tops
dandelion roots
2oz root ginger, bruised

2oz cream of tartar
2lb moist brown sugar
2 tablespoons fresh yeast

Fill a pan with nettle tops, put in a handful of well washed dandelion roots and the ginger, then fill up with water. Boil for about 4 hours, strain, then add the cream of tartar and sugar. Stir well. When cool, add the yeast. Leave overnight, bottle the next day.

Using 4lb nettles and 2 gallons of water, the recipe will produce 2 gallons of beer.

BALM WINE (a very old recipe)

1 peck of balm leaves
4 gallons water
fine sugar

4 egg whites
small piece of fresh yeast

Put the balm leaves into a large jar. Pour on the almost-boiling water. Let it stand all night, then strain. To every 1 gallon of liquid, add 2lb sugar, and stir well. Beat the egg whites well and add to the liquid, then put the liquid into a large pan. Heat, and whisk as it heats. As the liquid boils, skim continuously. Boil for 45 minutes, then put into a tub. When cold, add the small piece of yeast, whisking it in, and beat every 2 hours until it froths well. Leave it to work for 2 days, then put it into a fresh keg and cork tightly. When the liquid is clear, it can be bottled.

*   *   *

From Sowerby Bridge, a small industrial town in the narrow Calder Valley, comes the last word in drinks. After imbibing freely of the potent home-made stuff, the following recipe would come in handy.

SOWERBY PICK-ME-UP

1 pint stout	*½ pint rum*
1 pint brown ale	*½ pint strong beer*
8oz brown sugar	

Mix all the ingredients together and take 1 wineglassful 3 times a day. And if that doesn't pick you up, whatever will?

*   *   *

Yorkshire food, Yorkshire hospitality: both renowned, both taken for granted in the county itself. In the dark, grimy streets of my old West Riding, where touching the stone walls meant blackened hands, food was always a golden part of life, and although many of the recipes were plain and basic, they were filling, and warming. At feast days and holidays, there were the extras—the spice cakes and frumenty of Christmas; the parkins and toffees of Bonfire Night; and the sweets peculiar to certain districts, like Doncaster, home of horse racing and toffee.

DONCASTER BUTTERSCOTCH

½ pint milk	*6oz butter*
1lb demerara sugar	*⅛oz cream of tartar*

Dissolve all the ingredients in the milk, over a low heat, stirring with a wooden spoon. After a few minutes' cooking, drop a little of the syrup into cold water. If it rolls into a soft ball, remove the syrup from the heat and pour it into a well greased tin. Mark into fingers before it sets.

PLOT TOFFEE

1lb demerara sugar
4oz butter
1 tablespoon milk

4oz dark treacle
1 tablespoon water
1 tablespoon vinegar

Bring all the ingredients, except the vinegar, to the boil, stirring all the time. Keep boiling gently for 15 to 20 minutes, still stirring, until the mixture becomes brittle when a small piece is dropped into cold water. Stir in the vinegar, then pour into well greased tins. When nearly set, score deeply.

*   *   *

A Bonfire Night toffee from Swaledale, one of the wildest and loveliest of the Yorkshire Dales.

TOM TROT

8oz brown sugar
4oz butter

8oz dark treacle

Put all the ingredients into a pan and simmer for 30 minutes. When a drop crackles in cold water, the toffee is ready. Pour on to a greased plate, then work with the hands, pulling and twisting into long lengths, until the toffee is light and clear. Break into twists when cold.

*   *   *

For expatriate Yorkshire folk there can never be a place quite like it. We curse its cold sweeping winds whistling down the long valleys; the long winters before the first crocus; the rattling windows; and the struggle to keep the sheep alive on the fells. But when the sun shines over those fells, lightening the lime-stone crags, making subtle patterns on the darker gritstone, and we watch the clear becks and rivers splashing over brown pebbles, we know that we would not be elsewhere. The first purple saxifrage glows on the crags of Penyghent, the boots come out, and we are off to the hills of home.

Even the dirty towns are no longer dirty. There has been such a stirring of civic pride, and such a clean up of buildings following the Clean Air Act, that flowers now grow in those same streets, and the older citizens can sit and watch the strange comings and goings of 'them foreigners'. For one thing has never changed in Yorkshire. There are still 'us and them'; anyone born outside the county is a foreigner; and a person newly come to a village is called an 'off-cumed un' for at least ten years. But for all that, the welcome is still there, as firm and warm as always, and to anyone who comes to our beautiful county, we always say 'Nay, coom in, lad, tha's reight welcome!'

INDEX